MAGIC &
MEDICINE

FINDING THE WISE WOMAN WITHIN

JAYNE CRAIG
THE WELLNESS WITCH

MAGIC &
MEDICINE

FINDING THE WISE WOMAN WITHIN

First published in 2021 by Dean Publishing
PO Box 119
Mt. Macedon, Victoria, 3441
Australia
deanpublishing.com

DEAN PUBLISHING

Cataloguing-in-Publication Data
National Library of Australia
Title: Magic & Medicine — Finding The Wise Woman Within
Edition: 1st edn
ISBN: 978-1-925452-39-6
Category: Body, Mind & Spirit/Spiritual Healing/Magic Studies/Nature Therapy

Cover Illustrations: Kelli Savietto

This book is my offering to you —
wonderful reader —
seeker of magic in the mundane.
It is also an offering to
all of those who
came before me and
will come after me.

CONTENTS

CHAPTER 1

REBIRTH

*"We must be willing to let go of the life we planned
so as to have the life that is waiting for us."*
~ Joseph Campbell ~

My rebirth began as all births do. With mess, bodily fluids and pain. In my case the mess was my life, once beautifully mapped out, now in ruins; the bodily fluid was the tears that constantly flowed from my eyes; the pain was my heart breaking into a thousand pieces.

It wasn't just my heart that hurt. Every part of my body ached and my brain refused to function; instead it just played loops of the past over and over again, punctuated with moments of self-loathing and bitterness.

In early January 2018, I found myself collapsed in a heap on the floor of my room. I could smell the wool carpet underneath me, its distinct, wet wool aroma filling my nose each time my salty tears sunk into the pile. I couldn't stop crying even if I wanted to; sobs wracked my body and the tears came thick and fast. I sobbed so much I could barely breathe. I barely had the energy to drag my sorry form into the bathroom to vomit into the toilet each time the bile rose in my mouth. Once I'd finished, I'd retreat back to my patch on the carpet and curl into the fetal position to cry some more.

The reason for all this distress? My husband had called from his trip to Cuba to tell me it was over. We had been separated since April 2017, but he had been alternating between his home with us (me and our four children) and his 'other home' with his girlfriend in another country. When he came back for Christmas in 2017, we had discussed keeping the family together and getting our life back on track. I clung to this thread of hope as he left for a solo trip to the United States and Cuba. He promised me he would take the time alone to think.

He called me and it became clear that he was not alone. Instead, he was travelling with his girlfriend. When we spoke on the phone, his voice was so clear when he said, "It's over, we will never be husband and wife again." Those words, and the finality and coldness in his voice, will be etched into my being forever. With those words, something in me broke. I split apart at the seams; all my emotions, all the pain, all the confusion spilled out of me. There was no way to gather myself up again. I couldn't understand – did our twenty years together, our family of four amazing children, the memories we had created, the future we had plotted, mean nothing?

I would never be the same. The next year would be a year of deep depression, suicidal thoughts, intense anger, bitterness, begging and irrational behaviour, before I realised the truth of what had happened. I had been given an opportunity to be reborn and find my way back home to myself.

What followed this hellish year of despair was possibly the most beautiful gift I have ever been given; time. I had endless, glorious amounts of time to shape and fill as I pleased. I began my healing process. I had to get back to discovering who I was beyond mother and wife.

SERENDIPITY STEPS IN

Serendipity led me to finding a life coach, who helped me peer into the cracks of my marriage that I had previously glossed over. She helped me pull past hurts and self-destructive beliefs out of the closet I'd firmly locked them in. I used my Naturopathic skills to nurture myself and rebuild my nervous system, which was shot after 10 years of anxiety and a year of depression. I connected with some of the most incredible women and men who have enriched my life more than I could ever dream. Best of all, I reinvested my energy into the aspect of my life that had never left me, even when I neglected it: *my connection to spirit*.

I wouldn't change a thing about what happened with the marriage breakdown. It was horrific, but it was exactly what I needed, because without it I would never have left my marriage. I would have continued to give parts of myself away. I would have continued to twist myself into what I thought I needed to be in order to be the perfect wife, the perfect mother, whilst missing the mark every time. My then husband was the main breadwinner and I saw it as my job to keep the house and take care of the children, whilst cheering him on as he chased his travelling dreams and worked hard to pursue his business goals.

As a highly empathetic person, I naturally want to give those I love all I can, to not rock the boat and to make life as easy as possible. I didn't realise that this wasn't healthy or honest. I never realised that I was making myself sick trying to fulfil these roles. I never realised that my persistent (and, at times, extreme) anxiety and panic attacks, were like warning lights flashing on the dashboard of a car; they were wisdom from my higher self, using my nervous system to get my attention.

My inner wisdom made sure my anxiety was so crippling, I couldn't ignore the signals. I thought I was broken; I thought I was faulty. I didn't realise there was a connection between my anxiety and how alone I felt in my marriage. I was so alone – I was left to raise the children on my own most of the time while my husband worked on his business and took solo trips to travel the world. I was bored and alone, left playing a supporting role, watching someone else chase their dreams while I had very few of my own. I didn't realise what an impossible situation I had put myself in. I put all my hopes on my husband to make me happy, to be all things to me: husband, best friend, provider, lover, business guru, entertainer. I expected him to be the source of all of my joy and love, as well as the guiding light in the family. It was a lot of expectation and pressure on one person. I was expecting more of my husband than I was willing to give myself.

I grew more resentful of my husband, felt lonelier and less seen, as he worked longer and longer hours. Our relationship grew more and more distant and disconnected. Still, I never thought for one moment that our relationship would end. I had utter faith that we would pull through, that we were just in a rough patch.

It wasn't until my marriage was over that I realised the connection between my anxiety and my marriage. I was deeply and darkly depressed, but I wasn't having a moment of anxiety. I didn't have a single anxious thought or panic attack; this has remained consistent in the years that have followed. An epiphany struck...

> My anxiety wasn't because my nervous system was broken, it was because I was disconnected from myself and from life.

I wasn't living the life I needed, and my subconscious knew that. Our bodies are so wise, and mine knew what I needed even when my mind didn't. We ignore our bodies because instead we're tangled up with our thoughts and over-identifying with our emotions, focusing on the external instead of the internal.

THE SHADOW, THE SELF AND THE SOUL MATE

The simple truth is, I left myself a long time before my husband left me. I had stopped having my own life, stopped investing in my own happiness and instead gave that power over to someone else entirely. The man I once thought of as the love of my life was gone; he had made his choice to begin anew.

It took me a year of wading through a river of depression, contemplating and plotting my suicide, and of battling rage that at times made me so irrational and bitter that I didn't recognise myself. I would spend hours looking in the mirror, pulling every piece of myself apart, loathing my reflection, comparing myself to my ex-husband's new girlfriend, wishing parts of myself away. I would cry myself to sleep most nights, then wake up to cry in the early hours of the morning. When the children woke up, I would try and compose myself and put on a brave face. I didn't want my pain or the breakdown of their family to affect them any more negatively than it had to. I would try and remain calm and composed in public, or when I was around my children, but I would often find myself on the sidelines of my children's sporting matches, reading emails from my ex with tears silently sliding down my face, or bursting into tears if someone kindly enquired about how I was coping.

Through all this heaviness and sadness, I would have moments of clarity. In these moments, it felt like I was out of my body looking at my life and how things had played out. I could see my husband and neutrally observe how he must have felt, and perhaps why he made his decisions. From this neutral vantage point, I could see he was just a human, trying his best, trying to be true to himself. In those moments, although I felt angry and hurt, I was also strangely proud of him. Walking away from the life you've built to begin anew takes a certain amount of courage and conviction, especially when you know it will cause pain to many others. He did what I never could – he chose to honour his wants and desires, to put himself first. Of course, he made mistakes; we both did, and that is part of having the full human experience. I can't fault anyone I care for, for wanting to follow their heart.

This observer state is what I refer to as my higher self. It is the state where we are able to observe the self that has emotions, pain, pleasure and neutrally watch, unattached to the moment or the outcome. This self has no judgement, no fear, no blame. It just is, and its vantage point is one of pure love and connection.

In those moments of clarity, my inner self whispered a new truth to me. I wasn't in pain because my husband had found love with someone else, I was in pain because he didn't choose me. I felt like I was always putting him first and putting his needs ahead of mine. I was sure he would, in turn, do the same for me and put me ahead of his needs. He never did; he showed me throughout the relationship, over and over again, that he would put himself first and that he would *always* come first. These situations triggered my deepest fear and core wounding – that I wasn't enough, that I would never be enough, to be put first. This was an aspect of my shadow I didn't want to acknowledge or accept. It came from the wounding of a child who attended more than seven different schools and moved over and over again to new surroundings, new towns. It came from the child who struggled to fit in and find her place in the world. It came from the child who felt like she never got a say or got to choose where she wanted to belong. It came from the child who just wanted to be loved and accepted. I realized that I had to choose me, because no one else would save me.

One thing I've come to realise through this experience is that my ex-husband was not my soulmate, as I had previously thought. He was, however, possibly my greatest teacher, here to teach me some invaluable lessons. I was with him from a 18 years of age, until I was a grown woman at 37 years of age, and as such, I learned how to be an adult with him, as well as how to be a partner and how to be a parent. We travelled, built a home together and had many adventures and beautiful times. He was my first serious relationship and my first proper break up. Our marriage also caused me the most bone deep, earth-shattering pain I have ever experienced. I never knew how hard it would be to grieve for someone who is still alive, someone who you could reach out and touch, who you would choose over and over again, but who wouldn't choose you. I couldn't fathom how the heart could break and shatter in a million ways and yet still continue to beat. I felt broken and empty, and it took me some time to realise the truth. I needed this lesson, I needed to see how much of myself I gave away, and how diluted I had become. My shadows had to be seen and acknowledged in order for me to grow and be the person I was supposed to be. Ultimately, I realised my ex-husband, my teacher, gave me the most beautiful gift.

In breaking me, I was cracked wide open. He gave me back to me. In my healing, in reconnecting with my spirit, in rediscovering Jayne, I met my true soulmate. It turns out she had been with me this whole time; I just hadn't seen her every time I looked in the mirror.

FINDING MY MEDICINE

The road back to wholeness, to reconnect with my spirit and to rediscover who I was, was painful. It wasn't easy to acknowledge my role in what had happened, to look at my shadow self and not push away what I didn't like to see. It wasn't easy to stay neutral and to observe what was happening. My path was often very dark. I stumbled and fell many times and sometimes I contemplated not getting back up. The temptation to just dissolve into this nothingness of cosmic soup was often on my mind. Instead, I had to be willing to show up for myself, to accept myself and I had to be able to ask others for help. We are not made to do everything alone.

Looking back, I can hand on heart I say it was worth every moment. I truthfully wouldn't change a thing. The gift I was given, the gift I never wanted, gave me the happiness and wholeness I feel today. My life today doesn't even compare to the life I used to live, the person I used to be and this is the feeling I want everyone to experience.

This book is a collection of all that I used and continue to use in my daily life to heal and to bring myself back into alignment. It includes the rituals and practices I use to keep myself (and now my clients), listening and connected to inner wisdom. My hope is that this book provides you with stepping stones on your path back home to yourself, to your own soulmate within. I hope that these pages will help you to connect to your true nature – empowered, joyful, creative, magical and deeply loving.

We are made from stardust, and the wisdom of the universe runs in our veins. Our ancestors whisper their wisdom softly in our ears, whilst the creator of all is at work in our hands. We have all the magic and the medicine we need right here, inside of us. My hope is that this book will provide you with the way to connect with it.

Use this book as a framework, a building block, to give you ideas that you can take, personalise and make your own. There is no right way to walk a spiritual path; it is deeply personal and unique, and my way is not better than yours. I am not any more special or unique than you are. I do not know everything, any more than you do. We all have access to Spirit. We all have deep wells of inner magic and medicine inside of ourselves. Likewise, the ideas offered up inside these pages are not new. They have been influenced by the multitude of books I have read, the subjects I have studied, the people I've met, the places I've lived and travelled and the experiences I have lived.

I would also like to clarify what I mean by magic. I believe magic is all around us and accessible to us 24/7. I don't mean the *Harry Potter* type of magic. Magic to me is the fierce hit of a mother's intuition that saves her child's life. It's the many millions of actions the body carries out that keep us alive and functioning without any thought on our behalf. It's the fact that as humans we have a symbiotic relationship with strains of bacteria to keep our bodies healthy. It's the fact that our very cells are powered by mitochondria, an organelle that serves as a battery for our cells, as well as the cells found in plants and animals. Magic is also abundant in our ability to find love, wonder and contentment in our lives; in creative moments, in birthing new life and new ideas. Magic is also prophetic dreams, intuitive downloads, synchronistic events and the ability to manifest what we desire. In short, I believe magic is everywhere, in all facets of our life – we just have to open our eyes, our minds and our hearts.

If, as you read this book, you find yourself thinking, *I knew that* or *I could have written that*, that is excellent. It means you are already in tune with your inner wisdom. Think of this book then, as a reminder from the universe that it's time for you to start living your truth and practising your wisdom. Use the ideas presented in these pages as jumping off points, so that you can create a connection to the universe and to the riches that lie within you. Make these ideas your own; adapt them to suit your needs so that you can embrace your magic and your medicine. The world needs more of that and more of you.

Let's begin!

CHAPTER 2

HEALING

"We delight in the beauty of the butterfly, but rarely admit the
changes it has gone through to achieve that beauty."
~ Maya Angelou ~

When I was a young child, my favourite reading materials were folktales and fairytales from different cultures, including Greek mythology. I felt nature tugging and talking to me when I was out playing. The unseen was always playing at the edge of my vision; I knew that there was something else there, I just couldn't see it or articulate what it was. As a very young child, I remember seeing faces and forms in the dark, which often scared me. My parents put this down to a vivid imagination. Perhaps it was, but how was I imagining these things when I had no frame of reference for these forms I had never seen before? I grew out of seeing these images, but the gentle tug of Mamma Earth and the reverence for the spirit within nature stayed with me. I spent my childhood reading, playing in nature and immersed in the realm of my imagination, writing story after story.

I delved into the spiritual realm with my first pay cheque. I was 15 and my EFTPOS card was burning a hole in my pocket, so I went with a group of my friends and spent the weekend wandering around the shops in town to find something to buy. Down a side road was a small shop; in its windows, stained glass sun catchers and feathered dream catchers hung. Like a magpie drawn to sparkly things glinting in the sunlight, I stepped inside.

Incense wafted to greet me the moment I walked through the door. There were books, jewellery, little statues, and bowls of crystals on every surface. I had never experienced anything like it. It all felt so familiar and yet it was so foreign to anything I'd ever encountered. I picked up a few books and a crystal, and happily spent my first pay cheque. And so began my lifelong journey of learning about spirituality and healing. I visited that shop weekly, and spent most of my wages on books, crystals and other goodies. Even now, 25 years later, I still can't resist the lure of a good metaphysical shop and maybe one day I'll open my own little store of magic.

Finding the Magic in Me

When I was 17, my family moved and I found myself in a new town. I didn't know many people and I was at an awkward age where I didn't really want to interact with anyone. I found myself resenting my family's move and missing my friends. I was painfully lacking in confidence and, looking back at the signs I now recognise, I was depressed. There was one upside to the move – this new town had a great little crystal shop and the owners told me about a meditation class at the local healing centre. Intrigued, I went along.

This centre was in an old house. It was warm and cosy inside, the sunlight came pouring through the windows, the walls were lined with books that you could borrow, plants hung from the ceiling and that comforting smell of incense filled the air. From the moment I stepped through the door, I felt at peace. I would often go to the healing centre to borrow books, attend meditation classes, listen to talks on different topics, have my cards read or have a medium channel a message for me. I soaked it all up. In this alternative world of crystals, books and theories of spirituality, I felt like myself...and so much more. I felt expanded and connected to the world, through time and space, in a way that's rather hard to put into words. I dabbled a little in Wicca, Paganism, Buddhism and similar philosophies during my teenage years. For the most part, I hid this part of myself away for fear of being judged.

This thread followed me through the years, as I grew from teenager to adult. I cobbled together my own view on spirituality, borrowing beautiful ideals, rituals and practices from books and information I researched, reshaping them and making them my own. Underpinning it all was a profound reverence for nature, a deep respect for the knowledge of all cultures, a knowing that all sparks of life are all connected and that love underpins it all. The closest thing I found to describe what I believe is animism, the view that all things have a vital life force and energy and are therefore deserving of reverence and love. This includes animate and inanimate things.

I practised my version of spirituality quietly and in the shadows of my life, as and when I needed it or when I had time. I briefly put aside my crystals, tarot cards and books on witchcraft when I lived on a tropical island in the pacific with my then-husband and children. This was solely because the island's culture was religious and all magic was seen as "black magic" – meaning that it evoked evil spirits. I didn't want to make anyone upset or uncomfortable with my beliefs and practices, so I hid them away. Synchronicities and intuition were always present, but often I didn't acknowledge or pay them much attention. My intuition helped me save my eldest son from drowning when he was a young child; it helped me remain calm during natural disasters and make good investment decisions that helped me in the years to come. Synchronicities led me to studying Naturopathy and Herbal Medicine.

However, it wasn't until 2018 when my life as I knew it came crashing down around me and I found myself in a deep dark hole of depression, contemplating suicide, that spirit threw me a lifeline in the form of one singular thought: my children deserved a mother who was whole.

My children kept me going. I couldn't bring myself to leave and have them feel even one-tenth of the pain I was experiencing, so I had to do something about how I was feeling. I couldn't continue on as this depressed mess. I started using my Naturopathic training to improve my nutrition and I started using key herbal medicines to help my nervous system. It took some trial and error, but I found the right plant medicines for me. I was also on prescription medications from my doctor for a very long time. It was the right decision for me then, as I needed the breathing space the medication gave me. When I was ready, I began the long, slow process of weaning off these medications. There is no shame in taking medications when they are called for; modern medicine can work hand in hand with holistic health. I also began going to the gym and doing boxing to move my body as an outlet for the rage I felt, to get some feel-good hormones flowing and to meet people outside of my usual realm.

Next, I started working on my mindset. I hired Erika Cramer, a life coach, to help me get back on track and to hold me accountable (a big shout out to the Queen of Confidence, the brilliant Erika Cramer!). Because I was working on myself, loving myself, and rebuilding my relationship with myself, I started feeling a renewed sense of interest in myself and my old spiritual beliefs bubbled back to the surface. I threw myself into developing a daily spiritual practice that became the backbone of all that I do today. Occasionally I would stop doing this work for a few days to wallow and feel sorry for myself, and I think it's important to allow yourself these dips and not beat yourself up, but day by day my mind cleared and my spirit grew stronger. I worked on myself nonstop. I realised that the things that used to really bother me weren't that big a deal anymore. I'd catch myself when I got too involved in worrying about other people's thoughts, or if I was getting stuck in circulating thoughts, or if I was too self-critical or was stuck in a "poor me" mentality. I continually did things to push myself out of my comfort zone and tried things I had previously told myself I couldn't do. I took a huge leap and started sharing my journey with others. I met some wonderful new people and formed beautiful connections. About a year into intensively working on me, I found myself smiling and singing to myself as I went about my day. It dawned on me that I really liked myself; in fact, I loved and adored the person I had become.

ARE YOU STUCK? TAP INTO YOUR INNER MAGIC AND MEDICINE

If you feel stuck because of where you are at right now and feel disconnected with yourself, I want you to stop beating yourself up and start by honouring the place in which you find yourself. It doesn't matter how long it took to decide to rebuild your relationship with your inner self and Spirit, or how long it takes to rebuild that connection. We are always evolving and changing. The you that you were when you were a teen, or a young adult, or even last week, is not the same person you are today. You always have the power to change and to choose again. We are always learning; we get to change our minds and change them again, over and over. What matters is that you are here now, you always get to evolve, and you will always have access to magic.

I would like to suggest that you begin your journey of tapping into your inner magic and medicine by starting to record your thoughts. Crystals, plant medicine and manifesting are wonderful tools, but they will only get you so far. We need to be consistently working on our mindset too.

"Some people go through life trying to find out what the world holds for them only to find out too late that it's what they bring to the world that really counts."
~ Lucy Maud Montgomery ~

Manifest a New Mindset

Journaling is a great way to work on your mindset. You could begin writing in a journal or on your laptop, or recording a voice note or video of yourself. It doesn't matter which option you choose – the point is to start recording your thoughts and to have a way of documenting your journey. This is so important, because it allows you to do two things:

Firstly, you will be able to see growth, which you may not necessarily realise is happening at the time, but when you look back and see the reminders of what you used to do and think, and you can see how you have evolved.

Secondly, you will be able to see repeating patterns in your behaviour, your thinking and the situations you find yourself in. You will also be able to identify the ways your inner self is trying to get your attention, either by showing you the shadow aspects of yourself, or through little synchronicities, intuition and the like.

You may also like to use the same journal (or have another) to record your dreams, your meditation experiences, insights after card readings, rituals you come up with, and intuitive hits. It is always a good idea to track your progress when you start something new, be it a new mindfulness routine, nutrition plan, or whatever you choose to do, so you can record how you feel and track any changes.

I have included a journal at the back of this book so you can record your thoughts, feelings, guidance, reflections and intuitive 'hits'.

Writing out our thoughts and experiences also allows the mind to make sense of what is happening. Our brains are wired to look for patterns and to make meaning out of all of the sensory stimuli coming our way. Writing allows space so our brains can organise our experiences into a format that makes sense.

Having a safe space to write out your thoughts and fears, to allow yourself to be witnessed and seen, unfiltered and raw, just by yourself and the universe is a huge, healing step that is often underestimated. We all have a voice and a story to tell. The more that you can journal and record your life, the more deeply you will connect with yourself. Soon, as you write, you won't just be recording your thoughts and feelings, you will also be making space for your intuition and your higher self to start writing back.

The first time this happens is truly magical. One minute you are writing and all of a sudden, the writing becomes automatic and the wisdom you have always wanted and needed starts to flood out onto the page. Julia Cameron details a process known as "Morning Pages" in her book *The Artist's Way.* This an amazing outlet through which you can get in touch with your inner self; it allows you space to process the inner critic through writing out all of your fears. This then creates room for your inner wisdom to come through. The idea is that you create time and space in the morning to journal your thoughts without filter, in a stream of consciousness, and thought-dump for around three pages. Write absolutely everything that comes into your head without judgement. As you do this, you will see your inner wisdom; your higher self will start to write out advice or insight. Suggestions about how you can care for yourself, nurture yourself and help make your life richer and more fulfilled will come to you. It can even feel as though someone else is writing through your hand, because the information seems so different to what you have previously written.

Journaling daily will also provide you with insight into repeating stories or stereotypes you may find yourself buying into. When you notice these stories come up, ask yourself:

Is this thought mine? If not, who told it to me? Is it even a true story?

If you think it is true, how can you really know that it is true and in what ways could you prove the story is correct? These questions are based on 'The Work' of Byron Katie (thework.com) – they are hugely beneficial in questioning mindset and the stories we tell ourselves.

As you write, allow yourself to release all the stories, the emotions, everything. Writing is very cathartic; writing out our thoughts on the page allows our brains to organise and make sense of our struggles and emotions by putting them into story form. It is also important to allow yourself the space to tell your own story. There is huge power in telling your perspective and validating the experiences you have had for yourself.

I remember reading once that in our lives, we will all have times to play the hero or the villain in someone else's story. The idea that we could be the villain for someone can be a hard pill to swallow, but we don't get to invalidate another person's experience. We must be willing to allow them to have their perspective and the same is also true for you. You are allowed to tell your story; it isn't a case of laying blame on someone else's doorstep or being a victim, it is simply laying out your truth.

You may also like to gently allow the inner voice to answer your questions. Allow yourself to ask what you need, and watch for answers as you write. Perhaps it's a nap, maybe a hot drink, perhaps a walk in nature. Just write and allow your pen to flow – you may be surprised by the answers that come up. They could be very gentle nudges, or very clear bold language that explodes off the page.

This is your judgement free space to write and let go. This is your space to nurture and love yourself the way you truly deserve. This is the space where you can start to reconnect the threads of your intuition and higher self and stitch them back into the fabric of your life.

"Your intuition knows what
to write, so get out of the way."
~ Ray Bradbury ~

EXERCISE

Open up your journal or grab a fresh piece of paper, and start writing out what is bothering you. This could be a particular situation you are currently experiencing, an altercation with a colleague or a loved one, or perhaps a story that your inner critic is telling you.

- Write it all out. Explore every detail and every feeling. Allow yourself to be as petty, mean, or sad as you truly feel. Often we downplay how we feel or censor our stories and emotions for fear of being seen as dramatic or attention seeking, but this is your space to be exactly that! Think of the act of writing as a way to clean out the wound so it doesn't fester. Be detailed.
- Read back what you have written. Allow yourself to have a cry if you need to; let yourself feel all of your emotions.
- Spend some time taking deep, cleansing breaths. Have a stretch and a wiggle around. Release the attachment to any emotions that may have come up.
- Start journaling again, and this time, write out what you wished had happened. Perhaps you wish you had responded differently, or that you or the other person had behaved differently, or perhaps that you'd reached a different understanding.
- Now get still and centred. Feel yourself move into a neutral observer position. As you pick up the pen, I want you to write out what you need to hear now. Do you need to be told it is all ok? That you can choose again? That you are loved? That you are worthy? All of these things are true, but sometimes you need to remind yourself. You may find yourself writing out self-care suggestions that

will help you self-regulate and/or self-soothe. Allow your higher self to come into play and write out the wisdom you keep locked inside you.

- Once you are done writing, it's time for movement. Don't skip this part, it's hugely important! Put on some music and do some gentle twists and stretches, go for a walk in the fresh air, or put on your favourite tunes and have a boogie around your kitchen. This movement will allow you to gently twist and stretch your fascia (the layer of connective tissue beneath our skin that stabilises and separates muscles and our other internal organs), helping to move and release the emotions out of the cells of your body. Often we shove our emotions down and our bodies have no choice but to store these unresolved emotions, or express them in other ways. By incorporating movement into our journaling sessions, we can help to shift and release stagnant emotions.

CHAPTER 3

INNER WISDOM

*"Get smarter every day by listening to your
intuition, looking at the world with the eye of
your forehead. Jump, dance, sing, so you live
happier. Heal yourself, with beautiful love and
always remember...you are the medicine."*

~ Maria Sabina ~

How many times have you looked for answers outside of yourself? How many times have you quietly given your energy, your money, your power away by deferring to someone else; someone else who is more learned than you, who is in a more senior position, someone with a degree, or an expert in some area?

What if I told you that *you* were the expert? There is nobody on the planet more knowledgeable, more well-versed in the subject of you than YOU. You are the medicine. You are the truth serum, the energy barometer. YOU.

Let that sink in for a minute.

We are taught from a young age to look to others for the answers. Every time a well-meaning parent told us to deny our emotions, to not cry, to stop that tantrum, to be the good girl, we were taught how to act. We look to our teachers to tell us how to think, to healthcare providers to tell us the answers and to tell us all the ways our bodies are broken or letting us down. We need healthcare providers, but it is also helpful to check in with ourselves. Most of us forget to go within and check in with ourselves. We need to ask ourselves:

Does this information I'm receiving or being taught feel right to me?
Does it resonate and sit right in my gut?
Is my body trying to tell me something or get my attention through this illness or injury?
Are there unrecognised or unresolved emotions attached?

Louise Hay has some great information about health and the mind-body connection, if you want to delve deeper. We need to check in with ourselves a lot more than we currently do; most of us are running on autopilot or letting someone else run the show entirely.

TAPPING INTO YOUR INTUITION

Tapping into your intuition should be part of your daily practice. It's your innate guidance system, and in most people it's under-utilised. Much like strengthening any muscle in the body, your intuition will get stronger the more you use it. Journaling is a good way to tap into your inner wisdom. You can write out situations that cause you strong emotions, and gently probe into why you feel this way. You can investigate if there is a story attached to the emotion, and if there is a past hurt influencing this feeling or story. You can ask what it is that you need and then write out the answer with no judgement. You may want to envision a loved one, your inner mother or guiding angel. I like to envision a kindly wise woman.

Hold this image. Breathe deeply, then write.

What comes up for you?

....

....

....

....

....

....

....

....

....

Keep track of all your inner worries and your inner guidance in a notebook or a note on your phone and be sure to note when you prove yourself right! This can be handy to refer back to when you doubt your inner knowing. I have created a beautiful section at the back of this book so you can journal your experiences, feelings and thoughts as you read this book.

Meditation is a great way to provide space in your mind for clarity, calm and to hear your wisdom. Meditation has been proven to:
- Calm the activity of the mind
- Release stress and reduce anxiety
- Create positive physiological changes in the brain and nervous system
- Stabilise emotions
- Invite a sense of wellbeing and focus
- Enhance cognitive development
- Reduce feelings of depression, anxiety and pain [1]

I regularly use this imaginative meditation to tap into my inner wisdom.

~ WISE WOMAN MEDITATION ~

Get comfortable, put on some gentle music if you wish and close your eyes. In your mind, envision you are walking down a hallway. In your hand there is a key. This key could be as ornate or as simple as you like. As you walk, you come to a door. Take a moment and see the details on this door, is it simple and modern? Is it old? What material and colour is it? Notice now there is a keyhole, and that the key in your hand fits into this lock. Put the key in and turn it to open the door. As the door swings open, step over the threshold and into a lovely room, a room in which you feel utterly at home and at peace. Let the door gently close behind you. Take a moment and gaze around your surroundings. What shape is the room? Is it modern and airy? Cosy and cottage-like? Take a moment to really form the room into the kind of place you would love to spend time in.

For example, my inner room is large, with lots of windows letting in the most beautiful light. There's a fire with chairs arranged in front of it, and the walls are lined with books, art and plants. Across the room there is a slight step up to another smaller room and this one has coloured glass windows, a large table and shelves lined with potions, crystals and herbs.

Once your perfect room is fully formed, take a seat in one of your comfortable chairs. As you recline comfortably you hear footsteps. Your guide is coming to greet you. Allow yourself to receive your guide without any preconceived ideas. Notice what your guide looks like. Do they have a clear form? Are they male or female? Are they even human? How are they dressed? My inner guide is a short elderly woman, with amazing long silver hair arranged in two braids. As your guide gives you a welcoming embrace, notice the comforting, safe energy they give off. You feel yourself relax even more as you know you are completely and utterly safe here. This is your inner sanctum; it is only for you.

Now you and your guide have greeted each other you can start to tell your guide your problem. It might be an emotional problem or a physical problem. Listen for the wisdom your guide may give back to you. Perhaps your guide may just listen and make you a healing brew, or a soothing poultice. Perhaps your guide may just wrap you up in a blanket and sing to you whilst stroking your head. Let your guide give you the inner wisdom, healing and medicine you need.

When your guide has finished, know you have received what you have needed. Thank your guide and let them know you'll be back to visit them as often as you can. Stand up and exit through the door you entered through and put the key in your pocket for safekeeping. Walk slowly back down the hall as you start to gently move your physical body and come back to the here and now. When you are ready take a few deep breaths and open your eyes.

THE MEDITATION MESSAGE

You have just completed your inner wisdom meditation. How do you feel?

....

....

....

....

....

....

What wisdom or healing did you receive?

....

....

....

....

....

....

....

You may wish to journal your thoughts and feelings whilst they are fresh in your mind. Try and use this inner wisdom meditation whenever you feel in need of wisdom, comfort and healing. It is a beautiful way to help you feel connected to your universal guidance and to give yourself the love and comfort you deserve.

EXERCISE

The act of meditation can be really tricky. For some people, it is darn near impossible to sit still and feel serene. In this case, your mind may jump from thought to thought or the body feels twitchy and restless. Others still fall asleep - for me, meditation almost always ends up being nap time, despite my best intentions!!

Luckily we have a few alternatives, if you feel like sitting quietly in silent meditation just isn't for you.

- Guided visualisations are great because they give our minds something to focus on and they also engage our active imaginations, allowing our subconscious to come out and play.
- Active breathwork exercises, chanting mantras/affirmations/prayers or using prayer beads to help you count each cycle of breath/mantra/prayer are good ways to be mindful about your breath and body.
- You can try walking meditations or dance/movement meditation. If you feel like you're going to jump out of your skin when it comes to sitting still, an active meditation might be right up your alley. All you have to do is walk or dance with purpose, and focus on the present moment.

As you move, be aware of the following:
- Be fully aware of your body, the way your body moves through your space, and the sensations that echo up your legs as you move each foot. Think about the flush of heat in your skin as your body warms from movement. Focus on your heart as it beats in your chest. Be fully present with every sensation that runs through your body.

- Engage your senses—what can you smell? How does the air feel on your skin? What can you see and hear around you?
- Breathe with mindfulness. Feel your lungs expand and contract with each breath in and out. Note if it's easier to breathe through your nose or through your mouth (or both). Watch how your breath might change as you walk uphill or if the tempo increases as you dance.

You can even apply the above mindfulness prompts for movement as you undertake everyday activities such as folding washing, gardening or cooking dinner. Being *fully in* the present moment frees you from worrying about the past or the future, releasing you from the ties that bind you to the mundane and opening you up to receive insights and messages from yourself and the world around you.

CHAPTER 4

SPIRITUALITY

"There's a little witch in all of us."
~ Aunt Jet, Practical Magic ~

I am very proud of being a woman. Perhaps that is because I was fortunate to be born in a family and a culture without too much conditioning around what a woman should and shouldn't do. Although the messaging I got around income and power was fairly male-centric and I got the usual rubbish about how a "good girl" does and doesn't behave, I never felt unsafe or disadvantaged because I was born female.

I have always been aware of the power of the universe, of an existence greater than me, but it wasn't until I became a mother that I was given undeniable proof that there was something else. A consciousness exists, that you can give any name that you feel comfortable with; regardless of what each person calls it, it exists. Once you've witnessed the miracle of a child being birthed, or have grown a child inside of you for nine months. And then they come into the world beautifully formed, with their own distinct personality, you will know. To me, there is no further proof needed that a larger consciousness is at work, because it just gifted you with a unique new life to experience. Further proof is given at the other end of life, when you see a dying person or beloved animal take their last breath. You can feel the subtle change in the air, the almost imperceivable weight that suddenly lifts in the moment of death. That body of a beloved person or pet is changed; it is now undeniably flesh and bone. The spark that made that person, that animal, unique and full of character, that spirit that you loved, is gone. You can feel the change. That essence has gone from the body, returned to the cosmic soup, the universal consciousness, to the summer lands, to heaven, to paradise, whatever you believe.

If you are quiet, aware and open, you may still be able to perceive these beloved souls around you – it might be in the form of a comforting presence, a beautiful dream, an aroma, a song that is familiar and special to you, or perhaps in the form of a visiting bird or animal. The natural world shows us a pattern that repeats over and over. Life begins, it lives, it dies, its energy is reborn. We see this in the lifecycle of everything in nature; a seed germinates, it grows, it blooms, it fruits, and it eventually withers and returns to the soil, where it lives again as it nourishes the earthworms and fungi. If everything in nature is recycled and reused, why then would our spirits, our divine spark, not continue to live on and be reborn in another form? Why would we be the exception to the rule?

Women,* seem to be acutely aware of the cosmos, of the call of the divine. I think it's because we are the gatekeepers of life. Perhaps it's because, like the moon at its phases, we women are cyclical, our energy and emotions waxing and waning with our menstrual cycle. Whatever the reason, most women I encounter feel some form of spiritual

---

* Please note though I am using cisgendered references here, I am not in any way inferring that this is not inclusive of women who do not bleed, give birth or do not have a womb. I acknowledge and support the many ways to identify as a woman or to simply embody and experience femininity, but for the purpose of this book I am speaking purely from my own experience as a cisgendered woman.

pull. They feel the call to practise their own brand of magic, whether that be full-on witchy goodness – reading oracle cards and performing spells, gathering herbs and observing the moon phases – or just an interest in astrology or a love of crystals. Like Aunt Jet said in the movie *Practical Magic*, "There's a little witch in all of us."

SPIRITUALITY IS THE BEDROCK OF BEING

I still have books I purchased 25 years ago – books on crystal healing, past lives, Native American spirituality, witchcraft and magical beings. They helped shape my beliefs and expand my mind. I became more open to possibilities and open to others' beliefs because of these books. I became interested in collecting and using crystals for healing and in using different forms of divination. I learnt to use the pendulum, read runes and use tarot and oracle cards to help me hear whispers from my higher self. As I grew older, I travelled to different countries, attended group meditation sessions, kirtan circles and learned about Buddhism. Ancient cultures continue to hold a deep fascination to me. Travelling to Angkor Wat in Cambodia to visit this ancient structure and marvel at its jaw dropping beauty and energy was a huge treat for me, as well as a nod to my younger self who wanted to study anthropology. I hope to get to travel to more ancient sacred sights in my future.

My spiritual practice has become the bedrock for everything I do. Creating sacred space, celebrating life with ritual, leaning into my intuition and developing a relationship with spirit was vital to raising me out of a dark, suicidal depression and setting me on the path of self-healing and self-growth. When you experience the pain of a spouse or partner having an affair, it can really rock you to your foundations. This is especially true if the affair went on undiscovered for a large amount of time. It casts a shadow of doubt on all your memories. Were they truly authentic, just between you two, or was it an experience you were also sharing unwittingly with someone else? It is a cold way to realise that the only person you can really know is you.

What happens then, if you don't truly know yourself? If you've let yourself slowly dissolve into a relationship and your identity is tied up in that of the person whose web of untruths you now find yourself caught? If this happens to you, it can feel like you're living in quicksand, in a landscape where nothing is solid and the only thing real that you can hold onto is this one truth: that the only person you can really know is yourself. If you find yourself in this landscape, the way forward and out is through deepening your relationship to spirit and your commitment to healing and filling yourself up, following the path of communing with spirit and knowing self is where the true magic of life lives.

Spirituality is deeply personal. I feel we should all worship, pray or believe, in whatever way is in alignment with our inner self. We should live however we desire to be – loving, compassionate, and harmonious. We should embody a desire to work on ourselves so we are at our best, whilst acknowledging the interconnectedness of all beings; these practices can only be good for us. Whether you believe in one deity or many, the choice is yours. I personally find the idea that there is only one "right" belief system ridiculous. So many cultures around the world have beautiful ideas and at the core of all of them all seems to be love-centred living and compassion for others. I like the freedom to respectfully use what works best for me. Just as Eastern practices such as yoga and meditation are now commonplace and enrich many lives in the Western world, my practice has been influenced by many sources, many teachers, and many experiences.

That said, there is a difference between learning from different cultures and religions and taking inspiration from them, and outright appropriating what is not yours. In the world of spirituality, it can sometimes be hard to discern between what is inspiration and what is appropriation, because there is so much sharing of information in today's world. The best you can do is to learn with an open heart, have the best intentions, be willing to sit back and listen to others, and adjust and change when need be. To paraphrase Maya Angelou, "when you know better, you can do better".

If you, like me, learn from other cultures and other spiritual practices, be sure to acknowledge and reference them and support the work of those who are expert practitioners in those fields. There truly is so much to learn and there are so many perspectives to consider; you can never get bored on this journey.

I practise a very grounded type of spirituality. I believe that we are our own temples; the human body and soul is simply too amazing and complex to dismiss the idea that we have all we need for a connection to the divine, already within us. We don't need the trappings of ritual, or a special building to connect with the divine, because we have that connection within us at all times. However, it is true that a sacred space, a ritual, or a place set aside strictly for worship can help us to move more quickly from the mundane way of thinking and into a more expansive spiritual mindset. What if we took these tools we use to shift our mindset further? We live our lives as if the spiritual and sacred is very separate from the routine grind of our everyday lives, but they are not two separate things. There is magic in the mundane, wonder and Spirit all around us in all that we do, see, say and experience.

All that is required to express our beliefs, to worship, to move to a higher consciousness and to feel the love of the divine, is to look within and marvel at the wonder that is our human selves, or to go out into nature and feel the divinity and magic of Nature all around us. Spirit is always there; it never leaves us.

Personally, I think there is probably a masculine/feminine duality to universal consciousness. I think that every god, goddess, angel, saviour, and prophet is probably just a different expression of this consciousness. In much the same way then, every being in existence is also an expression of universal consciousness. Because of this I tend to call this presence universal consciousness, divinity, Spirit or just universe. But when you read these words, please just insert whatever word resonates most for you and your belief.

I like the idea that we are all just expressions of the divine, trying to learn and experience itself through different forms – be it human, plant or animal. When we pass on, we all return to a great cosmic soup of divinity. This is what allows us to feel the connection, the presence of loved ones after death, and the fact that we are never really gone, but continue to live on in a different form.

My youngest daughter once surprised me with her thoughts on this topic, when she came home from school one day at age five. She had been learning about water and how it can change from a liquid to a solid (through freezing) or a vapour (through heating). Watching me boil the kettle to make a cup of tea, she casually observed that she could see me in human form because like water when frozen solid, my essence was vibrating slowly and giving me my physical body. Once I died, my essence would be vibrating extremely fast because I would now be in spirit form – she explained that this is why I would no longer be able to be seen to her. She reassured me that, like steam in the air, I would still be around, but just harder to see. I was absolutely gobsmacked.

EXERCISE

The life we live is often very compartmentalised. The physical form is thought of as separate from our mental and emotional wellbeing; we separate these sides of ourselves. We think of ourselves as outside of nature and spirituality. We might see religion as its own segment that may only need attention on a certain day of the week or at special times of the year. A holistic perspective encourages us to see all of these aspects as very much intertwined. To reach a state of harmonious balance, we must give each area equal attention and acknowledge that an imbalance in one area will affect all other areas.

You might like to spend some time now with your journal, contemplating what Spirit and Spirituality means to you. Once you gain clarity on your beliefs, it is easier to form rituals and practices that help you to weave the essence of Spirit into your everyday life.

With this in mind, you may like to use the following prompts:

- What does Spirit mean to you? Do you have a specific deity or form in mind?
- Do you practise or are you drawn to specific religions or beliefs?
- Do you believe there is an afterlife? If you do, what do you believe happens in the afterlife?
- How are you currently nourishing and nurturing your physical, mental, emotional and spiritual aspects of self?
- How connected to nature do you feel right now?
- What are your daily practices?
- What would be your ideal way to feel each day?

• Do you believe you will be supported by Spirit and the world at large? Do you have trust and faith, or do you feel you need to control or force things to happen?

When you have written out your answers, spend time reading them back and reflecting on what you have written. Are there common themes? Can you see ways to build upon ideas to create meaningful rituals? Or, are there clear gaps that you can see that you would like to address by building specific practices just for yourself? For example, if you identify that the subject of death makes you anxious and uncomfortable, could you spend time watching nature and the interconnectedness of life and death within the natural world? Could you spend time learning about different beliefs, ancestor reverence or stories of connection with deceased loved ones or the angelic realm, in order to gain some clarity and comfort?

Use the information you have gained from your journaling to help build your daily personal practices so that you feel connected, calm and balanced.

CHAPTER 5

CREATE A HEAVENLY HAVEN

"Love is a little haven of refuge from the world."
~ Bertrand Russell ~

*H*aven. That word, the concept, always drifted around in my thoughts. Perhaps it was because as a child, I moved to a new town, new school and new house every three to five years. Perhaps it's because as a second-generation New Zealander, I felt a disconnect from my homeland and my roots. I felt this longing for a home I'd never seen and couldn't explain. I wanted a haven of my own. Later when I was doing my teacher training, I was introduced to a Māori word and concept *Tūrangawaewae*, which means a place to stand, or a place or places where we feel especially empowered and connected. *Tūrangawaewae* is our foundation, our place in the world, our home – that was the feeling I longed for.

As an adult, this feeling is what I want to create for myself and for my children. I want to create my home, my haven, my place to stand. We spend so much of our lives in our homes. Under its roof we shelter, we lay our heads, dream our dreams and live our lives. It bears silent witness to our lives as time ticks away. In the safety of our homes we laugh, we cry, we argue, we make love. Our home is a container for our lives, and we often treat it like it is nothing more than a dumping ground for our possessions, a place we sleep and eat and nothing more. Our homes can become messy, strewn with objects and clothing, collecting dust as we, busy humans, eat, work, sleep, repeat.

Mind-body expert and researcher, Dr Joe Dispenza says that our environments serve as a reminder that creates our beliefs about ourselves and therefore our reality. This is why it is so hard for you to change when your environment remains the same, as it reinforces old beliefs and patterns. For example, it is really hard to quit smoking if you are living in a home with other smokers or if there are cues all around the house that remind you of smoking. If it is true that our environment serves to reinforce our beliefs about ourselves, it makes sense to create a home environment that accurately reflects our infinite potential. It makes sense to make our home a place of aspiration, of joy, of empowerment, and a reflection of the divine.

MAKE YOUR HAVEN

I want to invite you to look at your home as I do – like a living being. It is a guardian that houses you and your family from the chaos of the outside world. Like a living being, your home deserves the best care. You don't have to be intense about it if that's not your thing, but a little bit of order, thought and care can transform your house into your haven.

When I clean my house, I clean with intention. I infuse the house with love; I weave my thoughts and wishes for joy and protection as I wipe down surfaces and clean the floors. I believe if I treat my home with care, it will shelter me with care in return. Every few days, I clean my floors with a spiritual cologne or essential oils, to not only make my floor shine but to do double duty and invite good energy in and seal my intentions. Every day, I open windows to let in the new day and let out any stagnant energy from the day before – even in winter, I open the windows for a few minutes in each room before I turn the heat on.

Your home is your sacred space. It is a reflection of you, so treat it accordingly. Fill it with colours, objects and scents that make you feel happy and inspired. You don't have to spend a lot of money or follow the latest interior design trends to make your space beautiful. Bringing nature in with potted plants, flowers picked from the garden or arrangements of foraged branches, pinecones, feathers or seashells. Allow your personality to shine through every object in your home. This is your safe space; your home is your place to retreat to when the day ends, or in times when life just seems too tough. You want to feel safe, seen and held the moment you walk in the door.

ALTARS ALTER YOUR CONSCIOUSNESS

I like to create mini altars on whatever space I have available – on the dining room table, kitchen countertops, dressing tables, on the floor. In these areas, I group objects together that I find beautiful or inspiring. It can be as simple as some freshly cut herbs, a candle and some dried chilli peppers on the kitchen bench – an arrangement that brings a smile to your face and does double duty, symbolising good health and protection to your subconscious and the universe. It could be photos of loved ones, a vase of flowers, crystals, objects of meaning to you, your favourite deck of oracle cards.

These altars are deeply personal and serve as a reminder that the threads of the cosmos run through every aspect of life, and that there is magic to be had in the mundane if we chose to see it and embrace it. They are a visual cue to your nervous system that it can relax and destress. They are also a visual cue to your Reticular Activating System, or RAS, which decides which information and stimuli in life is important to you. Altars help enhance the RAS in conscious and subconscious ways, acting as focal points of attention that create patterns and invoke beauty and joy. Thus these altars and spaces are training your brain to seek out more symbols of beauty and joy; the more you see, the happier and more joyful you become!

Altars can "alter" your consciousness, making it easier for you to commune with your higher consciousness, receive guidance, honour the divine and, of course, set intention of what you wish to see and create in the world. In addition to these mini altars, I also have two big altars: one that is my personal space to work with energies I want in my life, and one which is my ancestral altar for the whole family to use. Setting up altar space is easy and I find it to be a lovely and joyous way to express my connection to Spirit. You can set your space up by using the following steps.

SEVEN STEPS TO
SETTING UP SACRED SPACE

Step 1: Pick a place that you can see easily, but won't be disturbed by pets or other family members; a shelf or tabletop is great. Give this area a good clean and wipe down with a little Spiritual cologne, floral water or a carrier oil (such as coconut oil or extra-virgin olive oil), mixed with a few drops of your favourite essential oils. As you clean, send the space or surface blessings and good vibes. You will now have a clean, blank space to start creating with.

Step 2: Take a moment to pause and tune into the intention you want this sacred altar space to hold. What resonates with you in this moment of your life? Do you want to call in abundance? Self-love? Confidence? A place to honour your spirit and connect? Perhaps this is a space to honour loved ones who have passed, or to heal what has wounded you?

Step 3: Gather your materials – what calls to you and expresses how you want to feel? Is it fresh flowers, plants, crystals or items from nature? Or is it artwork, photos, statues, candles and oracle cards? What colours are associated with your intention, and can you incorporate them into this space? For example, you can use pink or red crystals and candles for calling in self-love or blue items for calm and connecting with spirit? You can be as elaborate or as simple as you like; this is your practice after all.

Step 4: Put on some music that you love to get into the vibe. Sing, dance and really *feel* what you want to create or call in. Light some incense, burn a smudge stick or diffuse some oils to further purify the space as you work.

Step 5: This step is the fun, creative part. Arrange your altar in a way that suits your aesthetic and is pleasing to you. You can move the items around and play with the set-up until you get an arrangement that makes your heart sing and puts a big smile on your face.

Step 6: Now that your sacred space is set up, take a few minutes to meditate and focus on the intent you wish this space to hold. Call it in and imagine your intent, or what you wish to call in is all around you in this space. Take a moment to really feel it, then bless it with gratitude.

Step 7: Check into your space daily. Use it as a touchstone, a place to come and check in for a few minutes each day and align with your intentions. Don't be afraid to change up items on your altar and move things around to keep the energy fresh and flowing, or even take everything apart and set it up for a new intention. This space is YOURS and is unique to you and your needs. There are no rules; this is your sacred space, where you come to discover your inner magic and medicine.

A HOMELY INVITATION

Every space in your home should be an invitation – a beckoning to the universe, to your deity, to the spirits of nature, to come on in!

Plants Matter – Because I view the world through the lens of animism, I'm a huge fan of bringing nature indoors. Potted plants are everywhere in my house. Not a single room is without a plant friend of some size and shape. I feel really attached to some of them, and have given them names. I love watching them grow, seeing them get new leaves and flower. I get a thrill out of trying to grow an unusual plant variety, or bringing an outdoor plant to live indoors. These plants provide beauty, they clean the air and provide oxygen and they boost mental health and compassion, just by being there and providing us with another living being to care for. It seems the feeling is mutual too; I've read research that suggests plants recognise and show preference for those who care for them.

The fun and expression doesn't stop once you've selected your plants. There's a variety of pots to suit your style; you can get creative with cloches and terrariums, or use tea pots, mugs or upcycled jars to reflect your style. I also like to collect moss and unusual looking twigs or rocks when I'm out walking in the forest to use as decorative mulch in my indoor pots. I always give thanks when gathering from nature, and never take too much. I also often place little sculptures, crystals and candles in the soil of my larger potted plants. Fairy lights can be strung through potted trees, or sun-catching crystals hung off sticks supporting plants that need it.

Did you know a study published in the Journal of Physiological Anthropology discovered that plants in your home or office can help you feel less stressed, lower of blood pressure and provide a psychological sense of calm and comfort.[2]

Colour and Textures and Motifs — You can also play with different colours and textures in your house; experiment with what really calls to you and invokes feelings of joy and contentment. Pick each photo and each object on display with love and meaning, so it brings a smile to your face. That's what we all want — a home that just invites good feelings every time you look at it.

Because I'm a real earth energy person, I like my home to reflect this love of Papatūānuku, or Mother Earth. Nature for me is extremely grounding, soul-nourishing and inspiring. Therefore, items found in nature such as feathers, birds' nests, and shells are incorporated heavily in my décor, as a lovely nod to the beauty found in the natural world. I have a vintage glass cabinet that a friend rescued from the rubbish dump that I use to store my nature treasures. It's kind of like an homage to the Victorian era curio cabinets. You could echo nature motifs in fabric patterns, colours and artwork. Using faux fur or nature prints on cushions, throws and rugs and even as table runners can continue to bring the outside in.

Interest can be added by utilising the ceilings to hang dried herbs or homemade smoke bundles, ropes of fairy lights or plants in glass bubbles. This décor adds to the cosy, inviting atmosphere of my home.

Witch balls also make for pretty window hangings. I was gifted a beautiful handblown glass witch ball that looks lovely in the sunlight. Witch balls are used to trap negative energies and entities and will apparently drop or smash when their job is done, so as beautiful as they look, try not to get too attached to them!

Sun catchers are also a favourite of mine. A lot of my windows have sun catching crystals and feathers hung with copper wire from driftwood. Seeing the sunlight play on the surfaces and rainbows projected onto surfaces makes me smile. Rainbows are reminders of our rainbow-coloured light bodies and are also a way to help infuse and boost our chakras. As a bonus, I also envision a little chakra balance and healing every time I stand in the rainbow light created by these sun catchers.

Crystals are another way I like to invite nature in. These stunning beings come in all sorts of shapes and colours, and each has its own individual and unique energy. Trust yourself to be guided to the right crystal at the right time. Though each type of crystal does have its own properties, what you feel from the crystal is important too. Trust any insights or intuition you may have. Pay attention to the way the crystal feels in your hand. My most potent crystal helpers make my hands feel tingly and magnetic, and the crystal feels heavy to hold, even when it may weigh next to nothing. Remember to cleanse and program your crystal once you get it home and always try to buy from suppliers who are ethical and sustainable.

CONNECT TO YOUR HAVEN

Now you have some ideas to get your creative juices flowing, you can go off and see what areas of your home need a little rearranging and TLC, in order to be the best environment for you and your family to feel uplifted, calm and in flow.

In making your home a haven, it is worthwhile to take some time to connect to the land you live on. Research the history of your local area – what was the land previously used for? Who were the original custodians or indigenous peoples to call this place home? How can you honour the history you find?

Try to find information on the plot of land your home is built on. Often we feel a pull to the home we choose to buy or rent. It is like the land recognises you and wants to call you home. I certainly experienced this for myself in my current home. I fell in love with this property the moment I saw it. It was uniquely built and large enough for all my children, but it was the land that spoke to me. Tucked away down a driveway, it had gardens big enough for me to keep chickens and it is surrounded by huge mature trees that were filled with the song of native birds. I felt safe the moment I stepped out of my car. After we had moved in, I embarked on a mission to turn the gardens into a permaculture paradise by planting many edible and medicinal trees and shrubs into the existing gardens. As I planted, I was pleasantly surprised to find mature fruit trees of different varieties tucked away in strange parts of the garden. Many months later I found out my home was once part of a much bigger property, on which two women biodynamically grew fruit and herbal plants to make organic skin creams and remedies for the community. This information absolutely delighted me because as a herbalist I was trying to do the same thing for my family and my clinic!

Many cultures have believed in elementals or the idea that each area of land has its own spirit. To honour and build a relationship to the land spirits and elementals, spend time lying or sitting on the ground outside, meditating and communing with the energy of the land. You may like to plant some special trees or gift the land an offering; perhaps a sculpture or a large stone or crystal. Hang wind chimes or bells in the trees to invite the air to play gently in your garden. Place a shallow bowl of water or a bird bath in the garden as an offering of nourishment for the local wildlife and to symbolise the element of water. Fire pits, braziers, pizza ovens or even candles can be safely and responsibly lit to invite the element of fire onto our land.

You may even like to find a special carving, sculpture, large rock or tree to become the representation of the guardian of your land and home. I have a gargoyle at my front door as my home's guardian to keep us safe and secure, and several sculptures of my region's first people, carved in traditional materials and forms, around the garden to watch over and honour our land.

EXERCISE

As we start to think about home as a haven, it can be helpful to consider the following:

- What makes you feel most at home and safe? Consider colours, sounds, scents and structure.
- What are your favourite features of your home? How can you emphasise these features to your advantage?
- Is there good sunlight and airflow in your home? If so, how can you take further advantage of this? For example, you could hang wind chimes that tinkle in the breeze of an open window, or position a comfortable chair to take full advantage of the morning sun. If the answer is no, how could you possibly rectify this situation? Think about trimming back trees to allow sun in, or putting safety latches on windows that allow you to safely leave the window open.
- What cues could you take from your local environment to bring warmth and calm into your home?
- What are some simple steps you could take to keep your home tidy and energetically fresh?

CHAPTER 6

THE SCENT OF SACREDNESS

"Smell is a potent wizard that transports you across thousands of miles and all the years you have lived."
~ Helen Keller ~

Think of how powerful scent is: a cologne you go weak at the knees for, a food that tantalises you, the familiar scent of a kind loved one. Our sense of smell is so important. It has the power to bring back memories, transporting us back to another place and time; it informs how we taste flavours in our meal. Scent can also invoke the air element into our homes.

Using sacred smoke, known as saining or smudging, is a practice long held by many cultures to ward off disease, repel negative energy or to invite in positive energy and bring on feelings of calm and wellbeing in those who inhale them. Plant materials, woods and resins have long been burned to invoke certain feelings and activate pathways in the brain and body. For example, frankincense is used in many different religious rituals. This earthy, spicy resin not only smells amazing, it also activates ion channels in our brain, helping to lessen feelings of anxiety and depression. Thus, when frankincense resin is burned, it helps people to relax and reach a state of wellbeing, the ideal state for people to be in when attending rituals or spiritual gatherings.

Burning candles can also help remove dust particles in the air. Certain aromatherapy oils and smoke bundles can help combat physical illness such as colds and the flu, because of their antiviral properties, whilst other essential oils can help open the airways to make breathing easier. Other aromas can be used to help us feel uplifted and refreshed when we feel depleted. Essential oils have to be used with care and with the right dilution, as some are not advisable for people who have certain medical conditions, during pregnancy or certain life stages, so due diligence is needed.

I like to use some form of scent every day, depending on my intentions. Some days I use my essential oil diffuser to uplift and refresh the vibe in my house. On other days, I light a few sticks of incense to refresh the air or as an offering to the universe. Every few days, I like to symbolically give my house a good cleanse of any accumulated negative energy to invite in new, positive experiences. I do this in one of two ways. Sometimes, I spritz the air and furniture around the house with a spray bottle filled with spring water and a small amount of floral water or a spiritual cologne, which is great when you're short on time, but big on intention. Sometimes, I light a smoke bundle and sain the house. When you are saining your house, it's important that you place your burning bundle in a heatproof bowl or container so that any burning embers can be safely caught, and always ensure good airflow with an open door or window. Some people prefer closed windows for saining but for me personally, I've found the smoke can become overwhelming and unpleasant, which takes away from my intent to bring magic into my life. Once the bundle is burning in a fireproof bowl, I walk through all the rooms in my house, gently waving the smoke with some feathers. You could also use your hand or let the smoke waft freely. Some people prefer to walk counterclockwise to expel negative energy in the house, but I believe your intention is what matters most, and you should just do what feels right for you. This is about bringing the sacred into your daily life so that you feel connected to the universe and empowered. There's no need to get hung up on doing things "perfectly".

MAKE YOUR OWN SAINING BUNDLE

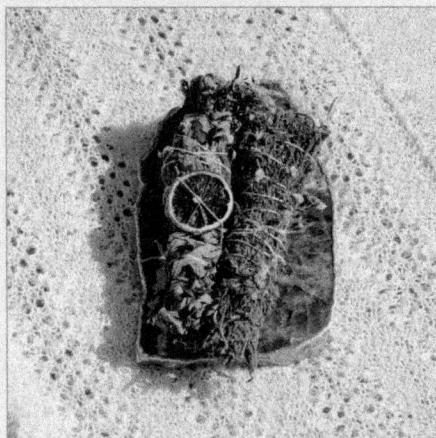

Many cultures have used smoke as a way to cleanse both people and their environment. For example, Native Americans burned sage and sweetgrass bundles; in South America Palo Santo is burned; Celtic peoples used Saining, a ceremony which combined the use of fire and smoke, as way of ritual purification of people, places and livestock. Burning certain plant materials also releases a pleasant aroma and can help cleanse the air of viruses and bacteria. You don't need to buy expensive smudge bundles from your local metaphysical shop; it's really simple and fun to make your own, and most of the plants you would use are extremely easy to grow at home in a pot or garden. Here's how you can make your own bundle:

Step 1: Gather your plant materials, after checking they are safe to burn. Aromatic plants like mugwort, lavender, rosemary, lemon verbena, lemon balm, eucalyptus, Virginia tobacco, white sage, cedar are good. Cut these plants to a uniform length.

Step 2: Bundle your plants together, into a size that seems manageable to you. If using Virginia tobacco, I like to use these large leaves to wrap all of the other herbs inside, but their scent is very strong, so a little goes a long way.

Step 3: Cut a length of organic cotton or thread and tightly wind this around your bundle, crisscrossing up and down the entire length. Remember plant material will shrink as it dries so it will need to be wrapped tightly. As you wrap, you may like to say prayers or blessings, setting your intention for the bundle. For a nice aesthetic look, you may wish to place lavender flowers or rose petals/buds on the outside of your bundle. You could also tie crystals, feathers or small charms onto the end of the smoke bundle you will use as a handle. Be sure to remove these items as the bundle burns down, so they don't burn.

Step 4: Hang your finished bundle in a cool, dry place with good air flow and out of direct sunlight. Leave them to dry – this may take a few weeks or a month, depending on the density of plant material used. Once your bundles are brown and feel crispy to the touch, they are ready to use.

Remember to always keep an eye on your bundles as they burn. Always use a fireproof bowl under your bundle to catch burning embers, and ensure good airflow as you sain, so the smoke doesn't become overwhelming to your senses.

IMBIBE YOUR HOME WITH GOOD VIBES

Some of my favourite products to use around the house are floral waters and spiritual colognes, such as Florida Water, which I was introduced to on my travels overseas. Spiritual colognes have a base ingredient of alcohol and contain a blend of dissolved essential oils, resins and herbs to create a distinctive pleasant aroma. There are also many floral waters, such as lavender hydrosol or rose water, which are readily available. Bear in mind that each floral water will have a different energetic property and therefore use, depending on the plant used.

What are spiritual colognes and floral waters used for?
- They can cleanse items on your altar or items that are new to you of any negative energy.
- Most floral waters and spiritual colognes have a pleasant aroma, so you can use them as a body spritz on your person, to bring feelings of balance and protection.
- Use a splash to cleanse your hands before tarot and oracle card readings and keep a bottle on the surface where you are doing your readings, to keep the area free of negative energy.

- For blessing your home with prosperity and luck, try cleansing your home with a mix of floral water and tap water. Use this mix to mop your floors and anoint your windows and doorways for protection.
- Bring calm and peace into your workplace or home by decanting a little floral water or spiritual cologne into a spray bottle (you can do 1/4 floral water/spiritual cologne and 3/4 filtered water to make it last longer) and use this to mist your home and your office.

These are just a few suggestions, and there are many more uses and plenty of wonderful articles and blog posts written on the use of spiritual colognes. There is also a rich history within many traditions, such as Hoodoo, Voodoo, Wicca and Santeria. Please take the time to research into the uses, so you can use floral water and spiritual cologne with respect and appreciation and not appropriation.

Sometimes spiritual colognes aren't readily available here in the Southern Hemisphere, so after a bit of research I came up with an Antipodean floral water recipe. It is inspired by some of the ingredients found in spiritual colognes and can be used in much the same way to cleanse your space and your spirit.

This floral water has similar aromatic properties as Florida water, so it smells lovely and familiar. The recipe utilises many dry ingredients easily found in the grocery store as well as many plants you may have growing in your garden or around you. Please remember when using fresh ingredients to use only spray free plant materials and to ask the plant's permission to harvest before cutting.

I believe that harvesting and making something from scratch allows you the opportunity to create something extra potent and powerful, as each step can be infused with your own energy, intention and prayer. Be mindful as you make.

You will need a slow cooker and the following ingredients.

~ ANTIPODEAN FLORAL WATER ~

Base ingredient:
9 cups of vodka (cheap vodka is perfect, as it is not for consumption.)

Dry ingredients:
3□5 sticks of cinnamon
2□3 tablespoons each of cardamon pods, cloves and star anise

Fresh ingredients:
Roughly 2□3 cups of each of the following; mint, lemon verbena, orange and lemon peels (roughly chopped), rose flowers (the more aromatic the better), jasmine, lavender.
Optional: Clove, jasmine and rose geranium essential oils (can be added in at the end).

Method:
1. Add all ingredients to the slow cooker. Put the lid on and turn on to low. Allow this mixture to gently heat and steep for 45 minutes, then turn the heat off and allow the slow cooker to cool.

2. Once cooled, strain the mixture through a muslin cloth-lined colander, with a bowl underneath to collect the liquid. Gather up the cloth and give it a good twist and squeeze to release any more liquid trapped in the plant material. The liquid can then be bottled and labelled for use. Make sure to add the date and the warning "not to ingest, external use only" on the label.

3. If you wish to add a bit more aromatic punch to the strained floral water, add in 15 drops of each essential oil to the bottle. Be sure to give the bottle a good shake before use, to make sure the essential oils disperse, as the oil will sit on top of your floral water.

4. The leftover macerated plant material can now be either be returned to the earth with thanks via the compost or returned to the soil around the plants you harvested.

If the above floral water isn't quite to your liking, you can use essential oils on their own. Just add a few drops of essential oils to your floor wash or in a spray bottle filled with water to cleanse your floors and surfaces.

If you are using a 100ml spray bottle, fill the bottle with 10ml of vodka, which is odourless and acts as a preservative, then top with filtered water. Add 20 drops of your chosen essential oil. Remember that essential oils are extremely potent and care needs to be taken to ensure they are not contraindicated in any health conditions, allergies and that they are suitably diluted. Never use essential oils internally; they are not safe for consumption. Some essential oils are not suitable for use around young children, infants or during pregnancy, so I would recommend thorough research.

Some suggestions for essential oils which could be used singularly, or together as a synergy, are:

Tulsi, Holy Basil, *Ocimum sanctum*: This top note aroma is sweet and spicy, like a cross between basil and clove oil. It can be used for mental and physical fatigue, and its strong scent makes it perfect for deodorising rooms and freshening pet beds. In ritual, Tulsi is used for protection, prosperity and abundance.

Lavender, *Lavendula angustifolia*: This floral middle note aroma is calming and helpful in reducing anxiety and irritability, as it balances out our emotions. It is also antiseptic and antiviral, making it a great addition to home cleaning products. Its scent is thought to help repel insects, so it can be helpful to diffuse during the summer months. Lavender oil has been used in rituals to help bring in energies of purification and healing, as well as raise sexual energy.

Eucalyptus, *Eucalyptus globulus*: The clean, fresh top notes of eucalyptus are antibacterial, antiviral, antiseptic, and work as a decongestant, so not only is it great for cleaning, but it's also wonderful for opening the airways during cold and flu season. Traditionally, it was used in magic ritual for purification and bringing about recuperation after a long illness.

Rosemary, *Rosmarinus officinalis*: The sharp, stimulating middle note of rosemary is helpful in stimulating the memory, relieving mental fatigue, clearing confusion and helping lethargy. Its pleasant aroma makes it helpful to clean and freshen surfaces. Magically, rosemary is used to invoke healing, common sense, self-assurance and protection. Avoid use if you have high blood pressure, epilepsy or are pregnant.

Lemon, *Citrus limonum*: This fresh citrus top note invokes feelings of happiness and joy. Its aroma is a natural mood lifter and helps to stimulate the memory and reduce fear. It is antiseptic, antimicrobial, bactericidal and insect repelling. The essential oil of lemon is thought to aid in enhancing psychic powers.

Peppermint, *Mentha piperita:* The top notes of peppermint help relieve feelings of nausea and aid clear thinking. It is also an excellent decongestant, so it's wonderful to diffuse when you are suffering from a head cold. As it enhances alertness, it's best not to use this oil before you wish to sleep. Peppermint is used in ritual to help create space for change or space to unwind when clarity is needed.[3]

EXERCISES

In order to find the right aromatics to enhance your home, consider the following:

- How do you feel about scented smoke? Do you find it overwhelming or do you enjoy it? Would you prefer saining bundles, incense sticks or cones or burning resins on charcoal discs?
- Do you enjoy using essential oils in diffusers, sprays or floral waters, or would you prefer to use scented candles?
- What scents bring you joy? What scents make you feel safe? Calm? Energised?
- Remember there are many simple kitchen items that you can use to bring scent into your life. You may wish to have a look in your kitchen and see where you can be creative!
- For example, rose water or orange blossom water that we use in cooking can make a beautiful freshening spray or a simple blessing water for you to cleanse your space with. Aromatic herbs such as lavender or chamomile can be steeped in hot water, strained, and decanted into a small spray bottle to make a calming mist (just remember to use these quickly, as they will spoil without a preservative). Spices and herbs could be mixed to make scented pouches or simple potpourri bowls.

CHAPTER 7

MAGIC IN THE MUNDANE

"You create your thoughts, your thoughts create your
intentions and your intentions create your reality."
~ Wayne Dyer ~

Our minds are wonderful, powerful things. They can help us or hinder us. Our thoughts have the power to enrich our experience, filling our lives with wonder and awe. They also have the power to keep us trapped and confined within limiting, self-sabotaging beliefs.

We have all probably heard stories of people who have suffered tragic life events and used the power of their mind to lift themselves out of the situation or have focused their thoughts on the moments of beauty available to them to bring comfort and joy. Likewise, we all probably know that one person who, no matter what opportunities come their way, will always find the negative viewpoint.

We can use our thoughts to focus on creating what we wish to see in the world, to help us feel wonder, joy and connection. It's from this place that we are able to take a compassionate view and marvel at all of creation, allowing us to focus on building a better reality for us all. I'd like touch on a few ways we can use our minds to work for us, instead of against us.

The law of attraction (LOA) is a popular concept that is based on the idea that like attracts like – that positive thoughts of love, abundance, vitality, will call in love, abundance, vitality, or on the flip side, negative thoughts will call in more negative experiences. In essence, your positive or negative expectations will cause life to present that very experience to you in your reality. Although I do believe that we attract in energies we actively cultivate, or repeatedly think about (positive or negative), the LOA that is talked about in today's society is actually quite problematic, often toxic and steeped in privilege. I would like to acknowledge this and clarify what I mean when I explore the LOA philosophy.

Typically, LOA maintains that you are responsible for your current reality. Every negative and positive experience belongs to you, because you called it in with your thought patterns. If you want to experience a better reality, then you need to clean up your thoughts to attract in what you wish to see in the world. This is relevant and true, to an extent.

If we follow this thought process fully, that would mean people are abused because they call it in, people die of cancer because they call it in, children suffer horrific situations because they call it in. No one deserves any of that, no matter *what*.

It's not someone's mindset that calls in abuse or a painful illness. The cause is either other human beings who inflict pain because of their own pain, genetics or just luck of the draw. Life is just like this sometimes; there is no rhyme or reason that we can see, at least not from our human positions. Life has always had its own agenda and, frankly, sometimes it sucks. People also have to be experiencing a certain amount of privilege in order to work on mindset. For example, you're less likely to give a crap about thinking positively and manifesting when you're in a war-torn country or struggling to survive. It is never okay to imply blame, gaslight or shove toxic positivity down someone's throat when they have been a victim of experiences that we can hardly comprehend. We don't get to invalidate another person's story or experience.

That said, I do believe that we can exercise a certain amount of influence over our lives by cultivating a positive mindset. If we are ill and still try to find joy and love in our life, then we are going to simply feel better than someone who is ill and stuck in a cycle of negative thinking. The hard and traumatic times in our lives often (but not always) give us profound understanding, skills and lessons we may never have otherwise learned. When I discuss LOA, please know I am not suggesting you are responsible for the cruelty the world may have inflicted upon you. I am suggesting that you have the ability to empower yourself through your mindset and you can draw more positive experiences towards you.

We also do have the power to attract certain energies and experiences when we focus on them. An example of this is one of those mornings when everything seems to go wrong: you wake up late, you stub your toe getting out of bed, you become frustrated and flustered, so you drink your coffee when it's too hot and burn your tongue. Then you drop your bottle of makeup in your rush to get ready, you struggle to find your keys, you get stuck in slow traffic on the way to work, making you late and you have to face the wrath of your boss. In this situation, the energy of frustration snowballs and picks up speed, turning everything upside down – until we get a moment to breathe, centre and realign our energy.

This idea of LOA is echoed in quantum mechanics theory, as shown by the double-slit experiment. In this demonstration, light and matter can display characteristics of both classically defined waves and particles, depending on whether the matter being fired through the slit was being observed or not. In other words, the matter being fired through the slits changed in accordance with the observer's expectation. There is also an experiment by French researcher René Peoc'h that involved newly hatched chickens that imprinted on a computerised robot. Prior to the chickens being hatched, the robot moved to the left and to the right side of the room in an even 50/50 split. His experiment then showed that chickens could influence the behaviour of the robot. When the chickens were introduced to one side of the room, their desire to be close to the robot they thought was their mother would cause the robot to move to the side of the room the baby chickens' enclosure was on *more frequently*. The even 50/50 split went out the window! The baby chicks' collective desire to be next to the robot they imprinted on appears to have influenced the movements of a robot!

Sympathetic magic entwines and works on the same ideas of LOA and quantum theory too; objects that symbolise certain things can be used to call in what you would like to experience.

Since the dawn of time, we have used sympathetic magic to call in what we want to experience in our lives. Think about the sculptures of old gods and goddesses, each of which embodied different virtues, strengths and powers. People would then use these deities to symbolise what they wished to call on and draw those energies into their lives. For example, fertility goddesses were used to ensure an abundant harvest or a pregnancy. Simple items like protection amulets, or the idea of a love potion, are all aspects of sympathetic magic. Even a vision board or altar could be viewed as an aspect of sympathetic magic. I like to harness LOA by creating spell boxes, jars or bowls. It's fun, creative and if you imbue your creations with focus and intent, it can be very powerful!

Dr Joe Dispenza speaks about the power of intention in his work on the placebo effect. He suggests that when you assign intention, meaning and purpose to what you are doing, you will produce a greater result. This is powerfully simple, and incredibly wondrous. It is so empowering to know that we have the ability to co-create with the universe.

We humans are also equipped with a Reticular Activating System (RAS), which helps us with calling in the LOA. This hugely helpful system is a network of neurons located in the brain stem. It is responsible for taking what you focus on and creating a filter for it. Your RAS will take all the incoming data you are constantly bombarded with and sift through the data to present you with only the pieces that are important to you. For example, your RAS will take the importance you assign to your name and alert you when you hear your name in fragments of conversation. Your RAS is also the reason why you suddenly start seeing a certain thing that you want everywhere.

We can harness our RAS to help us use the law of attraction to draw in what we wish to see and what we wish to manifest in the world. An easy way to do this is by assigning meaning to certain colours, objects or symbols and then using them to repeatedly signal to our brains that we wish to see this in our everyday life; this is essentially sympathetic magic.

I rely on the power of symbology heavily in my everyday life. I have assigned meaning to certain colours, images, animals, and plants. Much like we can all understand that a smiley face emoji symbolises happiness or see an image of a heart and think of love, these symbols elicit a certain meaning or emotion in me when I see them in my life.

Many signs, symbols, colours, animals, and the like have been used as symbols throughout history, and continue to hold the same meanings to this day. Having a good book on symbology is really helpful and I would also encourage you to keep your own notebook that lists what certain colours and images mean to you. This will then become your own language with the universe – a way that your higher self and spirit can communicate with you. You can then take note when you notice certain symbols or animals visiting you in dreams, in cards you pull or just randomly crossing your path in daily life. You can gain a deeper insight into what is going on in your life and your psyche, or gather guidance from the universe.

COLOUR MAGIC

⚝ BLUE ⚝

• Sky blue often symbolises self expression, peace, wisdom, calm, trust and freedom.
• Darker blues symbolise honesty, loyalty, inner security and the spiritual self.

Use Blue to promote feelings of calm, relaxation and security in your surroundings. Blue can be worn or used to reduce stress, promote and inspire feelings of trust, order and harmony.

⚝ RED ⚝

• Red symbolises passion, vitality, love, excitement, danger, courage and commands attention.

Use Red to stimulate the senses, draw attention to yourself or to objects. Red can give you a confidence boost and a dose of courage. Red in your surroundings can create a feeling or urgency, fire up passions and even inflame anger.

⚝ GREEN ⚝

• Light green symbolises growth, harmony, health, fertility, abundance and kindness.
• Dark green symbolises harmony, stability, balance, nature and safety.

Use Green to restore your energy when fatigued. To promote feelings of nurturing, rejuvenation, relaxation and healing. Green can help you to feel abundant and balanced.

⚝ YELLOW ⚝

• Yellow represents fun, happiness, confidence, enthusiasm and positivity.

Use this colour to lift your mood, boost your energy levels and give yourself a confidence boost. Yellow's stimulating properties make it a helpful study aid.

⚝ ORANGE ⚝

• Orange symbolises optimism, independence, creativity and fun.

Use Orange to encourage creative flow, expressive freedom and spontaneous fun. Orange is also a mood booster, promoting happiness. Much like red, orange also invites and holds attention.

⚝ PURPLE ⚝

• Purple is associated with royalty, religion/spirituality, imagination, sensitivity, compassion and also mystery.

Use Purple to invoke a sense of luxury, to aid psychic development, and to inspire the imagination. Purple helps you to tap into your inner wisdom and power.

SYMBOL SEEING

When you feel stuck in life, a great exercise is to take a blanket and lie out in the grass to do some cloud watching. As you lie there, allow yourself to feel cradled and held by the earth. Feel all the stress drain out of you into the warm grass, to be transmuted into something more positive by Mamma Earth. Let your mind wander as you softly focus your gaze on the clouds that are drifting through the sky. Take note of the images you see in the clouds. Jot them down in a notebook for easy reference later, or record a voice note on your phone. Are you seeing certain animals in the clouds? Are the images forming a story as each cloud floats through the sky? Be sure to look up the symbolism of the animals or images you noted in the clouds. There will be whispers of wisdom from your consciousness in those images and symbols divined in the clouds.

You can also use this exercise to look for symbols in soap suds as they swirl and circle the drain of the shower, or in the patterns of wood grain in furniture and flooring, or in the residue of coffee grains, or tea leaves inside a mug. The latter two are known as the art of Tassomancy or Tasseography, and there are many great books on the subject should you wish to delve into this realm further.

I love to create symbols just for me; they are "my" signs from the universe. This is particularly helpful if you want reassurance that you are on the right path or making the right decision. Choose something to become *your* symbol – nothing too ordinary that you would see every day. Choose something slightly unusual and be open to seeing this symbol in unexpected ways. You may see it in words on a sign, motifs on a fabric, in jewellery, on book covers or in the background scenes of TV shows, hear it in song lyrics, or see it in stuffed toys, in works of art or in photos that crop up on your social media feed.

The topic of symbology is a fascinating and vast area to delve into. Colours, numbers, animals, plants, all have their own specific and unique meanings; whilst psychologists like Carl Jung have insight into how our psyche uses the power of symbols to communicate through dreams and imaginings. Myths and legends are also a great place to gain more insight into symbology and how it was used to impart meaning and wisdom. I would highly recommend you invest in a few different reference books to help you unlock the meanings behind the vast array of symbols you may encounter. These books will come in handy for all manner of things; dream interpretation, tarot reading and for everyday interactions that may catch your attention.

To help get you started I have included a few basic symbols/images you may regularly come across in your dreams or daily life. In addition to any meanings you may research, you may also create *your own* interpretation and/or gut feelings about these images. This will give you extremely valuable insight.

Man: Masculine self or a man in your life. The conscious self.

Woman: Feminine self or a woman in your life. The unconscious self.

Child: Innocence, co-creation, union of the masculine and feminine.

Skeleton: Your true self. The core of what always remains. Ancestors.

Angel: Higher self, divine guidance. In the case of archangels; each will have particular traits and associations linked to them, and a quick Google search should net you plenty of information as to what they might be. For example: Archangel Michael is linked to protection, leadership, cutting ties to toxic energies.

Nakedness: Purity, free from shame, comfortable in your own self.

Key: Unlocking the true self, knowledge and wisdom

Animals: Our wild, untameable self, Nature. In addition, each animal will have unique traits and qualities dependant on its type, so further research will be needed to understand its individual symbology. Here are a few to get you started:
  – **Lion:** Solar energy, lifeforce, masculine energy, animal nature.
  – **Horse:** Divine self, strength, endurance, loyalty, strong of heart, what forces maybe currently driving you.

- **Serpent**: Kundalini energy, knowledge, goddess energy, animal nature.
- **Dog**: Signifies a once wild animal which is now a tame and loyal friend, harnessing our wild natures to be of use to us, instead of taking over our lives. Guidance from that which will never leave you aka God/source/universe.
- **Bird**: The ascension of the soul, messengers from Spirit. Each type of bird will have its own assigned meaning, again an internet search or a good book on symbology should be able to help you dive in deeper.

Water: emotions, fertility, creativity, stream of consciousness we all have access to. Note whether the water is calm or rough, flowing freely or stagnant, as this will give you insight as to how you may be processing your emotions and/or creativity.

Emerging out of water: Birthing of consciousness, early development of self, instincts.

Moon: Emotions illuminated, cycles, intuition, shadow self, goddess energy.

Sun: Masculine, vibrations of light, life force, collective knowledge.

Star: Life power, guiding light, pure energy of light that is within us all.

Tree: Knowledge, ancient wisdom, the embodiment of the adage "as above so below". Each tree species will have its own special symbology, it is also helpful to take into account the age of the tree, number of branches, if it has fruit, flowers or if its devoid of leaves. The shape of the tree (e.g. is it bent and bowed or does it stand tall and strong) as this will give you further insight into its meaning.

Mountains: Symbolises the hard work we must put in in order to overcome obstacles, to get to our goals in life, to be able to see with a different perspective, being closer to hearing the voice of Spirit.

Paths: The road or journey that you are taking. Winding or paths that undulate symbolise life's ups and downs and twists and turns.

Coffins: Limiting beliefs, the boxes you keep yourself in. The limits of the physical plane.

Stone walls: Truths we build our reality on. Protection. What are we hiding behind?

Throne: Wealth, material, status, authority.

Crown/wreaths: Victory, success, manifestation.

Lamps/lighting: Illumination, light at the end of the tunnel, shining the light for others.

Chains: What binds us and keeps us prisoner in our bodies and emotions. Limiting beliefs. Loose chains indicate you can free yourself if you wanted to.

Spirals, circles, infinity symbol: Balance, renewal of energy, never ending cycles.

Your Own Signs are Signs

I'll give you an example from my own life: my universal symbol is the peacock.

Growing up, I admired peacocks' beautifully coloured feathers, but I very rarely saw them in physical form or even in artwork. After my divorce, I needed inspiration to find my voice and to start taking up space, and the image of a peacock with his huge tail fanned out came to mind. The peacock was taking up as much space as he pleased, inviting others to look at him. You can't not look at a peacock; his beauty is too stunning and you can't ignore his loud, wailing call. The peacock was the perfect symbol for me and my new mission to take up space and embody all that is me. I was so committed to embodying the peacock energy, I tattooed one on my shoulder!

I simply asked the universe to show me a peacock if I was on the right track, or if I needed a nudge to keep on going, a kind of gentle love note from the universe. Then the fun started!

I received an email from a jewellery maker I loved about her new animal talisman design rings; the one that featured in the email was a peacock. I'd be watching TV and a peacock print would be on the bedsheets of the main character's bed, or the feather motif would show up on a book cover. I visited a friend and as we drove to a crystal shop, we went past a road with the name Peacock in it. We pulled up to the crystal shop, out in the country, to find peacocks roaming the car park. I'd scroll through social media and see peacocks in people's photographs and videos; peacocks would show up in the most unexpected places with the most uncanny timing.

When I was trying to decide whether or not to commit to publishing this book, I was deep in a mindset of not-enough-ness and imposter syndrome. I asked the universe: "I don't know what I'm doing; I don't know if I can write a book that will be of service to others. If writing a book and going with this publishing company is for my highest good, please show me a peacock in the next 24 hours."

That night I was checking social media and a Facebook Marketplace ad was in my feed. The item for sale was a duvet cover set featuring a motif of peacocks! I told myself it was just a coincidence, as I put down my phone and settled in to watch a TV show. During the episode, the main characters went to a vast English country estate. As the scene progressed, they parked their car and a peacock casually strolled across the lawn. As the characters started their conversation, the peacock's cries could be heard in the background for the next two minutes of the show. I felt the universe knew I was being dismissive and was trying to drive its point across!

I paused the TV show and laughed and laughed, and then called my friend to tell her what had happened. I couldn't write any of these experiences off as coincidences – the universe was trying to tell me something.

The universe hadn't finished with me though. The next day, as I got on the video call with the publisher to speak about my idea for this book, Susan was showing me some covers of books that she and her company had recently published. I was absolutely astounded when one of the books she chose to show me was by an author called Rita Barbagallo, who is also known as "The Red Peacock". Not only was I taken aback by her name, the book cover featured a gorgeous picture of her holding two large peacock feather fans! The universe had shown me exactly what I'd asked for, multiple times in the 24 hour timeframe. I felt like the universe knew exactly how big a decision this was for me, so it was showing me peacock after peacock so I didn't get lost in excuses or rationalisations.

I have so many other stories like this, and they truly bring me great comfort and joy. We could say it's just our RAS looking for signs and symbols that we assign meaning to and looking for the information when we need to see it, but that doesn't make it any less magical. The fact that we have a system in our brains that is able to look for symbols, that is able to co-create a language with the universe, to see signs and symbols and divine personal meanings from them – I choose to see that as further proof of a conscious universe that wishes to communicate with us so we know we aren't alone. Life is more vibrant, more special, and more connected when we look for and embrace the magic held within the mundane. We are our own oracle, and we can divine the information we need to enrich our lives. We limit ourselves because we often don't trust ourselves or the information we get. We question whether we're worthy of knowing the answers and receiving the messages from Spirit. But really, why wouldn't we be? We are all connected and the threads of Spirit run through us all, so use your natural intuitive abilities to enrich your life. You just need to decide what your personal symbol–your love note from the universe–will be and trust it when you see it.

There are multiple ways to get our RAS working for us and to connect with the universe through sympathetic magic, LOA, quantum mechanics theory, manifestation, or whatever you wish to call it. At the end of the day, we are simply working with the universe and our higher selves to call in what we wish to see manifested in the world, for our highest good. It's important to add that caveat, as we often ask for things we think will make our lives better, but we don't always have the foresight to see if what we are asking for will be right for us or serve us and our loved ones long-term. Sometimes we need the hard lessons and the pain to get to the gifts we never knew we needed.

Here a few examples to prime your imagination and harness your RAS. Get those creative juices flowing, and create some sympathetic magical goodies for yourself.

Spell Box for Self-Love

During a period of self-healing and growth after my divorce, I naturally felt quite lonely. I didn't want to fill that gap with another person. I wanted to be okay, to be happy, with being complete just as I am, so I decided to focus on self-love.

I bought a small red chest from the craft store (around 5cm long) and filled it with the following objects, whilst visualising total love and joy in my own self.

- A small carved wooden heart, on which I wrote the word *love*.
- A dried red chilli pepper, to symbolise feeling passion and excitement in my life.
- A small cutting of ivy, symbolising an eternity of love, friendship and fidelity.
- A small rose quartz, the crystal associated with the heart and love.
- A tiny jar of honey, symbolising the sweetness of life and good health.
- Rose petals, as the rose has long been associated with love.

This spell box now sits on my bedroom altar. I see it every day and it gives me the daily cue to love myself – fully, joyfully, as I am, regardless of whether I'm single or in a relationship.

SPELL JAR FOR CALM

There was a period in my life when I was riddled with anxiety, so I created little spell jars I could keep on my dresser, or slip into my pocket to remind me that I would be okay. They reminded me that I could create the calm I wished to see and feel. When I was anxious, I'd hold the tiny jar in my hand and focus on its contents until the anxiety passed.

Craft stores and dollar shops are good places to find little jars that are only a few centimetres high; these are perfect for spell jars. In my jar, I placed:

- A very small, rolled up piece of blue paper, with the word "calm" and the symbol for peace written on it.
- Lavender buds, for calming and protection.
- A pinch of Withania powder for strengthening my nervous system and stamina.
- A small piece of blue lace agate to help me go with the flow of life and enhance feelings of relaxation, calm and peace.

Focus on feeling calm, releasing anxiety and being perfectly safe. Visualise being wrapped in a beautiful blue blanket of peace, as you fill your jar with the items. Place the stopper in the jar. Seal the stopper by pouring over melted blue or white wax. Once the wax has hardened, you could carve in the peace symbol or a sigil or word that symbolises calm to you. Place the jar somewhere you can see it daily, so it will remind you to breathe in calm and serenity.

ABUNDANCE BOWL

I always keep an abundance bowl on my personal altar. This bowl is designed primarily to bring in money, but also positive energy, kind thoughts and deeds, moments of gratitude and sweetness, and things that make you feel rich and abundant, physically, emotionally and spiritually. When you create this bowl, focus on what abundance means to you. Focus on the feelings and freedoms abundance brings, and the peace of mind you have when you know your needs and your family's needs are taken care of. Focus on how good it feels to share with others. Ask for abundance to be drawn into your life with ease and for the highest good of all.

To create your abundance bowl, you will need:

- A crystal bowl, like those ones your grandparents had for fancy dinner parties. You can find them easily in thrift stores. Because they are traditionally thought of as special occasion homeware, they are perfect for harnessing that abundant feel. Alternatively, you could use a green bowl, as green is the colour of abundance and money.
- A large white pillar candle.
- A selection of crystals traditionally linked to abundance; pyrite, carnelian, Congo citrine, jade, and a few pieces of clear quartz to amplify your intention.
- Dried herbs that are also tied to abundance. Chamomile, lavender, cinquefoil, pieces of apple and some comfrey leaf are good to bind the abundance to you.
- Glitter or mica in gold and silver, if you like sparkles!
- Coins, dollar notes, and the like. I like to use a variety of currencies to signify wealth coming from a variety of places.

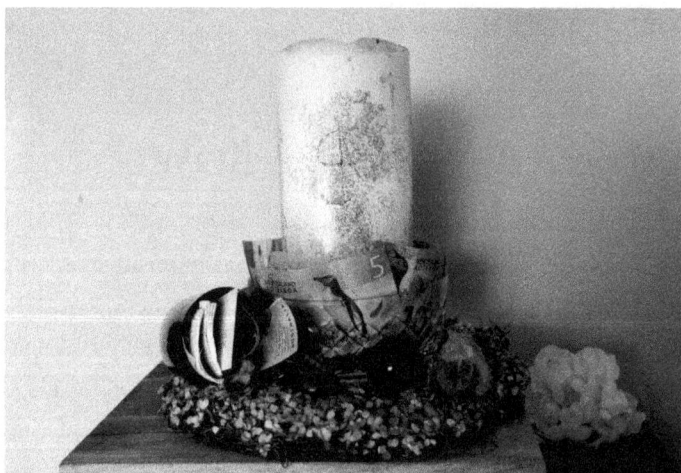

Whilst visualising what abundance means to you, pick up your candle and write words such as abundance, wealth, gratitude, and joy on it. You could also carve money symbols into the sides of the candle. Once done, rub glitter or mica into the carvings. Place the candle in the middle of your bowl, then place your money, dried herbs and crystals into the bowl, anchoring the candle in place. Place the bowl on your altar or somewhere you can see and visit it daily, perhaps on your office desk or family dining table. Every day, light your candle and spend a few moments visualising abundance coming your way and giving thanks for all the good and positive things that flow into your life. I like to periodically "feed" my bowl with more coins, dried herbs and crystals, to keep the energy flow fresh and consistent. I also replace the candle when it burns down. I never take money from this bowl, and the kids also know to look elsewhere for loose change. The money stays there as an energetic gift to the universe.

VISION BOARDS

Vision boards are another way to invite the vibes you want in your life into your home and your life. You can make them as large or as small as you like; you can make one or many to place around your home. You can make them out of paper or canvas, put them in picture frames, or use whatever you have on hand.

Vision boards are a direct expression of your creative soul's yearnings to the universe. You can draw, paint, and use photos and cut outs of words and images from magazines. Place these objects in a visually pleasing way on your medium, so they form a visual story or mood board of what you would like to welcome into your life. It could be representations of the ideal career, travel, financial wealth, specific material items, love or family. Don't be shy with your imaginings. As you create your vision board, play music that helps you get into the vibe and really make it a passionate experience so you infuse the whole making process with your wishes and intentions.

Once completed, place or hang the vision board somewhere you can see it every day. That way your RAS will receive this visual cue every day, even if you're not spending time consciously looking at the board. You could also create digital vision boards and use them as wallpapers on your phone or laptop.

Mini Vision Boards

I also often use singular oracle cards or Major Arcana Tarot cards as mini vision boards. Simply take a bit of time to quiet your mind, look through the Major Arcana and choose a card that resonates with where you currently are in your life journey, or that represents where you would like to be. For example, The Magician Card is good for focus, action and success and the Empress Card draws in fertility, self-love, creativity and nurturing.

To make an altar space, clean an area that will not be disturbed, such as a shelf or a table, and cleanse and prepare your space. Place your card in the centre of your altar space, or somewhere you can see it easily. Looking at your chosen card, pick out the colours you see and find objects that could represent them on your altar. You can add candles of the same colours as well. If you don't have coloured candles, white tea lights or candles will do the trick.

Looking at your card, find some objects that you feel resonate with the spirit of the card's archetype. For example, if your card has actual foliage or flowers depicted, perhaps create a small posy of these plants to place on your altar.

Statues, figurines or photos that depict the archetype or animals shown in the card can be incorporated.

A bowl or jug of water can be used if your card depicts lots of water imagery, or a jar of dirt for earth energy, incense sticks for air energy etc.

Use objects that symbolise the archetypes' energy you wish to harness. For example, a journal and pen if you wish to write a book, money for abundance, a rose for self-love, or a bottle of supplements or a piece of fruit for health are perfect examples.

Crystals that resonate with the card's energy can also be added to the altar space.

Place your chosen objects around the altar space so that it makes a pleasing arrangement. You may wish to bless your space by offering some sacred smoke in the form of incense, resins or a smoke bundle; use whatever you prefer.

Return to this space daily to spend a few minutes connecting with your chosen card, perhaps lighting a candle, journaling, meditating or just taking a few centring breaths.

Your altar space can be kept for as long as you need or desire to work with it. When you are done, simply give thanks for your lessons and healing and dismantle the altar. You can then repeat the process with other card archetypes, as and when you want to. This is easily the most fun way to use the tarot archetypes; as a bonus, it helps deepen your relationship with and understanding of the tarot.

EXERCISE

Before making your vision board consider the following:

- What is your intention? What do you wish to draw into your life? Get crystal clear and focused.
- What words best describe or go with this intention? For example, if your intention is abundance, these words could be: money, wealth, freedom, joy, security, plenty, gratitude, harvest, fortune.
- What colours do you associate with this intention? Sticking with the abundance theme, they could be green, yellow or gold.
- What symbols or pictures could you associate with your intention? Be sure to use ones that make you feel good and in flow.
- How much space do you currently have, and what resources do you have available to create with? This will help you decide between making an altar space, a vision board, a mini vision board or a digital board.
- Gather your materials, put on some music and light candles to set the mood and get creative! Remember this is your creative vision for your life; you are creating to get into sacred flow state, to harness the LOA so don't worry about others or their judgement. Create solely for you and for Spirit.

CHAPTER 8:

THE MAGICAL WORLD AROUND YOU

*"She had so deep a kinship with the trees,
so intuitive a sympathy with leaf and flower,
that it seemed as if the blood in her veins was
not slow-moving human blood, but volatile sap."*
~ Mary Webb, Gone to Earth ~

Plants are one of my favourite things to talk about. I'm a total Earth Mamma, my sign is the earth-based Virgo, I'm trained in permaculture and herbalism, plants are inked onto my skin and my home is filled with plants, both inside and out. I love nature; I need to be around and connected to nature every single day.

There won't be any high-rise apartment living for me; the thought of space travel or spending long periods of time sailing the ocean fills me with horror. Give me soil, flowers, trees, and animals, and I'm happy. The feeling is mutual – nature is good for us, soothing our nervous system and healing our physical and emotional pains.

The Japanese ritual of Forest bathing (shinrin-yoku) has been shown to alleviate stress levels; the soil has been shown to release bacteria that is antidepressant and makes us feel happy.[4] The earth wants to nurture us. She wants a relationship with us too.

With that in mind, plants can really make a difference to your living space, whether you're growing them outdoors in the garden or inviting them into your home.

Plants are beautiful to look at, and can help improve the quality of air in your home, filtering out toxins which could potentially become breading grounds for bacteria. NASA has stated that house plants can help destroy viruses too.[5] Plants are also incredibly soothing to our nervous system, so having access to a garden or keeping plants indoors is a wonderful way to destress and relieve anxiety.

We can also learn a lot from our plant allies. Plants communicate with each other non-verbally, via chemical signals and sharing information and nutrients with each other through underground mycorrhizal networks. Research has shown trees show preference to other plants in their genus, blocking nutrients from other tree varieties and sometimes making the soil incompatible for other species to grow within the area they share.

Although trees tend to not touch each other in forest environments, in order for optimal photosynthesis, some trees can form strong bonds with one another. These trees intertwine their root systems and grow in such a way that both trees lean towards each other, their branches often touching or interlocking to form archways. Trees will also send nutrients to other trees that have been cut down, in order to keep the stump alive. Plants have their own intelligence and teachings that they will freely share with humans, if we care to sit and listen.

If we spend time observing and sitting with plants, we can learn to lean into becoming more in flow with the seasons, as well as learn ways to communicate our needs beyond just using speech. As you spend more and more time with plants, you will learn the subtle differences in each plant's energies and begin to notice what plants make you feel good and at ease, simply by being in their presence. This is how our ancestors learned about plant medicines. Certain plants have also traditionally been planted or used to bring joy, health or protective energies to homes and the people that dwell within them.

You can build a relationship with plants by sitting with them in meditation, picking sprigs to place under pillows for dream work, by caring for and observing them throughout the seasons, and through drinking them as tea or adding them to your food if they are edible. You can learn a lot from observing a plant growing! I've had many plant teachers over the years as I studied herbal medicine, some of which helped me with my anxiety and some which helped me ease my heart break. I learned one memorable lesson through a hop vine I bought to grow in a pot and climb up the side of my house.

When I first planted this vine, it was tiny, only six or seven centimetres high. I had visions of harvesting the hop cones for dream pillows and anxiety tinctures, and eating the tender shoots in the spring. I planted the vine in a huge pot and as it grew larger and larger, I trained it to grow up the side of my house. The pot was placed near the outdoor hose, so every time I wanted to water the garden, I had to lean close to the vine to turn the tap on. The hop vine has very rough stems; every time I got close, no matter how careful I was, the vine would hook onto my skin and cause nasty, itchy, red welts across my arms. I grew to hate that vine – I thought it was out to get me!

One Autumn, I was cutting the dead growth of the vine back and noticed that even though the pot was large, the roots of the hop plant were growing out of the bottom and trying to anchor into the dirt below. With a bit of effort, I dragged the pot into the chicken yard and planted the hops next to a dead tree, so the tree could provide a framework on which the hops could climb. The next summer, that hop vine was rampant. It grew so large, climbing through other fruit trees I had planted, festooning them with chartreuse-coloured hop cones and gifting me with more medicinal plant matter than I could ever hope to use.

Here's the interesting thing – even though I had to go under the hop vine to water other trees and plants, the vine never grabbed at me or caused welts. Towards the end of summer, I was harvesting some hops to dry and I was meditating with the plant. I was given this imagery of the parallels between the vine and feminine energy. The cones of the hop vine are soft and soothing to the touch; she is beautiful and graceful to look at as she weaves through the trees. Juxtaposing this, her vine is tenacious and coarse, and she will leave welts on your skin if you venture too close without caution and respect. This is the ultimate reminder of feminine power. Women can be soft and fierce, gentle and tenacious and must always be approached with respect and reverence! The hop vine also taught me a lesson. The difference between growing with restriction in the pot, versus growing with wild abundance where no restrictions were in place and only a support framework was given, was incredible. This mirrors the human experience. How often do we confine ourselves with rules and fear of judgement and then wonder why we do not thrive? What would happen if we freed ourselves from a self-imposed prison?

There are so many plants and trees out there for you to develop relationships with; there are so many teachers waiting to gift you with their lessons.

Specific plants can be helpful in bringing certain energies into your home and garden:

Aloe Vera, *Aloe barbadensis*: Aloe is a delightful plant to grow indoors as it often thrives in pots. She is also a wonderful plant to have around due to her healing abilities. If you suffer from sunburn, minor burns, abrasions or simply want a soothing face mask, aloe is the plant for you. After asking permission, break off a part of her leaf, and squeeze out the soothing gel and rub onto your skin. The aloe leaf will seal up where it was cut, so you can harvest a few leaves and keep them in the fridge during the summer months so that you always have some soothing aloe gel on hand for irritated skin. Energetically, I find aloe to be kind of like a mamma bear – her spiky leaves offer protection, whilst her soft centre is soothing and gentle.

Lavender, *L. angustifolia*: Lavender has a wonderful, calming scent. She is also extremely useful and medicinal. She is a great plant to grow if you suffer from headaches or bouts of irritation, because you can go outside, run your hands through the stems and flowers of the lavender bush and get a little free aromatherapy!

You can also harvest the heads of lavender to use in soothing baths or dry them to place under pillows to help lull you into sleep. Lavender has long been used in rituals for healing, purification and protection; she is always the first plant I put in the gardens of any new home I move into.

Lipstick Plant, *Aeschynanthus radicans*: Come to my house and you will see a beautiful lipstick plant hanging from my ceiling, happily growing with lush abundance. Although I've nicknamed my plant Rapunzel, I get a distinctly masculine vibe off this plant. Perhaps it's because the flowers, which look like tubes of lipstick, also bear resemblance to a part of the male anatomy! This plant has a really happy, confident energy and so I like to keep him in my home to encourage this energy in myself and my children.

Monstera, *Monstera deliciosa*: I adore this big plant for its stunning foliage and its big energy. I have three of these large plants in my home, one of which I'm as attached to and treat as a dear friend. She is actually my favourite – don't tell my other plants!

Monstera is another plant that feels very protective in its nature, as its large leaves help to shade other light-sensitive plants that grow beneath it. If you brush up against monstera in the morning, you will notice little beads of water will fall to the ground. This release of water from the monstera's leaves will help to keep the soil moist and in good health. It is because of this generous action that I associate monstera with abundance and vitality. I've potted several monsteras and keep them throughout the house, in communal areas and at the front door, to invite abundance and the spirit of generosity into my house.

Mint, *Mentha*: Mint will grow vigorously in the garden and easily spread, so it's a good one to keep contained in a large pot. You can get many different varieties of mint and it is one of the best plants to grow as it makes a delicious tea that helps settle digestive issues, reduce headaches and improve clarity.

Mint tea is also wonderful for when you get a bout of cold or flu, as it helps relieve congested sinuses. Because mint grows so abundantly, it is thought to bring prosperity into your life as well as giving you clarity of thought.

Mugwort, *Artemisia vulgaris*: This wonderful plant has long been associated with the goddess, lucid dreaming and psychic development. She grows rampantly and wildly in the garden. To me, she invokes feelings of wisdom and grace. Her growing habit is upright and tall, and I often nibble a small amount of her leaf when I need to clear my mind and get back in touch with my inner wisdom. I also will keep a bunch of mugwort by my bed or place dried mugwort under my pillow when I wish to do dream work.**

Sunflower, *Helianthus*: This is one of my favourite flowers; just looking at it invokes a sense of cheerfulness. Sunflowers can be grown in the garden or in pots, or enjoyed as a cut flower. They symbolise loyalty, friendship, confidence, joy and longevity. Because you can enjoy the bloom of the sunflower and eat and plant her seeds, the sunflower is also linked with nourishment and abundance.

Sunflowers also have the ability to draw toxins out of the soil and still produce a beautiful flower, which reminds us that we too can draw upon our toxic or rough experiences and still create a beautiful and abundant life.

Rosemary, *Rosemarinus officinalis*: This beautifully fragrant plant is associated with memory and can be very helpful to have around the house if you or your family are studying. Simply pick a sprig and crush its leaves as you study to bring focus and clarity of thought. You can then use the scent of rosemary to help you recall the information you have studied. Rosemary is also a plant of protection;

** Please note: this plant is not suitable for pregnant women.

it is one of the plants the famed herbalist and hero of mine, Juliette De Bairacli Levy, claimed should always be in the garden and on hand for herbal remedies.

We all want our homes to be safe and secure environments, to house both ourselves and our families, as well as our hopes and our dreams. The following is a list of easy-to-source plants that have been historically linked to bringing a protective energy to our homes. There are plenty of wonderful books out there, such as Scott Cunningham's *Magical Herbalism*, or Juliet Diaz's *Plant Witchery*, that you can refer to.

Plants for protection: angelica, acacia, ash, aloe vera, bay laurel, basil, cactus, clover, cypress, fern, fennel, geranium, lavender, lemon verbena, mugwort, nettle, rosemary, sunflower, yucca.

If you are interested in working with plants, I suggest finding a select few that interest you to work intensely with for at least a few months. Grow them in your home, research them and find out the historical and modern day uses, as well as the myths and legends they may have associated with them. Meditate with them. Care for them. If they are edible or medicinal, make teas or meals with them. Ask the plant to visit you in your dreams and to work with you. Do not hurry or rush the process. Offer the plant love and respect and you will be amazed at the wisdom you get in return.

"You are magic.
Don't ever apologize
for the fire in you."

~ Unknown ~

CHAPTER 9:

SELF-LOVE

"To fall in love with yourself is the
first secret to happiness."
~ Robert Morley ~

Let's focus now on our relationship with the self. Our viewpoint about our inner self and our physical body is often tangled up with feelings of self-loathing, inadequacy, comparison, and rejection, combined with an unhealthy amount of other people's opinions. We look to others to fill the holes, fill in the flaws we think we have, and to make us whole. It's not our fault – we are fed the myth that that perfect someone who will complete us is out there; this idea is reinforced over and over again, through stories and movies.

The truth of the matter is that we are whole and we are perfect, just as we are. Whole. Perfect. We are our own soulmates. All we need to do is wake up to this truth and start the journey back home to ourselves.

I want to give you an alternative narrative. We are born into our physical bodies, but as I've touched on before, we have a higher self. This higher self is not dependent or contained within our physical bodies or this physical realm. You can call it your higher self, your soul, your spirit – whatever word works for you. What if this longing for a soulmate, this partner that will complete you and make you feel whole, is actually a longing to complete yourself, because deep down you know there is a part missing. It's not another person as we have been taught, but a longing for a full-bodied connection to all parts of yourself, your physical self, your shadow self, your higher self. You, in completion, are literally the soulmate you are yearning for.

That's not to say a romantic partner isn't wonderful – we can definitely feel that soul recognition from connection with others, through platonic or romantic relationships. We just don't need another person to complete us. Connections with others will be better and richer because you feel complete within yourself. You are not putting pressure on someone else to be everything and everyone to you. I know I've made that mistake in the past, and it wasn't fair on anyone. I often felt really alone and unseen because of it.

I often listen to talks from Ester Hicks as she channels wisdom from a collective called Abraham. I once heard Abraham-Hicks say the following, which really stuck with me. She said, "If you're craving stability and belonging, but you can only feel these things whilst holding another's hand; do you really think you feel safe, stable and belong? What happens when that hand is no longer there to hold?"

When I heard that, it really resonated with me because I have always needed that hand to hold.

All through my life, I was dependent on others. I depended on friends, family, and my ex-husband to validate me and give me direction. When I was young, my family moved around so much, which led me to always depend on my parents to accept and validate me because I didn't have access to a secure friend network. When I met my ex-husband at the age of 18, he was a lot older and more experienced, so I naturally differed to him. I became caught up in trying to be the perfect partner, and then the perfect wife and mother. I started to value his opinions over mine, and slowly that eroded my sense of self. I wasn't a mindless puppet by any stretch of the imagination, but I wasn't a well-rounded, whole person either.

After my marriage broke up, I found myself living entirely on my own terms for the first time in my life, raising my children by myself, decorating my house how I wanted, and making decisions without anyone else weighing in or giving direction. It was both liberating and hugely terrifying. Every single decision (or indecision) was on me, and often I was paralysed with fear that I would get it wrong. Then it dawned on me – there is no wrong, only experiences and lessons learned. If I wanted to trust myself, I had to get to know myself. When I got to know myself, I learned to truly love myself. It didn't matter if I was surrounded by people or completely alone; the one constant was always me, and that was the relationship I had to prioritise.

In order for us to become fully autonomous individuals, we have to explore every facet of our personalities. We have to dive into self-love. We have to learn our strengths, our weaknesses, our shadows as we wade through the muck and messiness within the complexities of being a divine human. By doing this, we learn how to love ourselves in our wholeness. At first, this may sound selfish, or narcissistic. But truthfully, in finding true love and reverence for ourselves, we cannot turn away or deny the spark of divinity in another. If we revere ourselves, we will be able to revere another; if we honour and cherish our unique traits, we will love and defend another's right to express their unique traits and quirks too. This is how we can reach wholeness as individuals and as a community.

When we think about the people we love, it's often because they make us feel a certain way. We love the way they treat us; they make us feel loved, special, protected, or we love the feeling of fun, passion or excitement the other inspires in us when we are around them. Those feelings can diminish over time, and when stressors hit, or irritation at little quirks sets in, it can be hard to feel the same intensity of love for that person because we are dependent on that person making us feel a certain way.

I want you to think about the love you feel for your pet, such as a dog or a cat, and the love you receive back from them. We love our pets because they are cute and cuddly and make us laugh and our animals love us for the food, shelter and belly rubs we give them. In addition to this, we also often have deep bonds with our animal companions because they love us unconditionally. When we are mad or sad or even neglectful, those treasured animals of ours offer us loyalty, devotion and pure love we often don't feel from humans. Because the animal has no ulterior motive and no judgements, they don't care if we show up for them perfectly made up and emotionally pulled together, or as un-showered, tear-stained, emotional wreck in our pyjamas; the pet is complete in itself and it just loves you for you.

With the above in mind, I invite you to spend some time journaling on old patterning, old beliefs, and opinions about you and the love that you deserve. Think about any hurts and lacking self-love that have wormed their way into your soul and taken up residence in your mind.

Journal prompts to consider:

Do I love and cherish the body I'm in? If so, how do I show this love?

Do I compare and judge myself and/or others?

Do I listen to my body's need to move and need to rest?

Can I look into the mirror with ease and do I like what I see?

Am I holding onto old hurts or unkind words?

Am I in a loving, kind, healthy relationship?

Do I believe I'm worthy of love?

Do I love myself and/or others unconditionally?

Can I give and receive love with ease?

Whilst journaling, it is also worth looking at our relationship to love and sex, examining if we feel they are one and the same or if they can exist separately. Look at how you allow yourself to give and receive pleasure, the quality of orgasms you enjoy, the feelings that sex and intimacy brings up. Sex is magic – an energetic exchange in which we can build energy (with a partner or solo) to call in what we wish to see manifest in the world. A healthy attitude towards sex and pleasure is part of the joy of being fully human and nothing to be ashamed of, and yet we all too often have trauma or shame mixed into our sexuality. If you do notice some unhealthy or negative patterning surrounding sex, chatting with a therapist or somatic healer that specialises in the realm of embodied sexuality can be helpful in dismantling these patterns.

Once you have finished journaling, you will want to release those thoughts which no longer serve you. You may wish to write these thoughts out and safely burn the paper, or make and create your own witch worry doll.

WITCH WORRY DOLLS

A witch worry doll is inspired by those beautiful little worry dolls you can often purchase in shops, mixed with the idea of smoke purification.

Worry dolls originate from the Indigenous peoples of Guatemala. My research suggests that parents or elders would traditionally give worry dolls to anxious or fearful children, in order for them to release their worries by talking to the doll and placing it under their pillow at night, so they could wake the next morning, refreshed and unburdened. I think that is such a beautiful way to give voice to our thoughts and release the weight we have been carrying.

This witch worry doll is bigger and can be made out of aromatic plant materials you may have growing in your garden or nearby. We all gather resentments, hurts, thoughts and fears that burden us along our life's path. Worry dolls are a beautiful way to allow us a safe space to offload these burdens, and symbolically release them into the universe. If we wish to embrace ourselves and love ourselves fully, we need to let go of the hurt and fear that weighs us down. These worry dolls are made out of plant materials that have their own potent power to give the dolls a little magical boost. You can also have fun creating a ceremony out of burning the dolls when you are ready to release and let go of that which no longer serves you.

~ MAKE YOUR OWN ~
WORRY DOLL

You will need:

- twine or string
- a selection of aromatic plants
- a pair of scissors

Suggested Plants:

Mugwort: Mugwort has long been associated with the moon, women and witches. She will grow and multiply easily in any garden. Mugwort is a brilliant herb to help enhance intuition, sharpen focus and enhance clairvoyance; it is also very protective.

Cedar: Cedar has been my mischievous teacher of late, and has a special place in my heart. For me, its aroma invokes memories of my grandparents, as well as, more recently, a link to a dear herbalist friend who lives oceans away. Cedar is protective, and aids in healing. Its smoke is also used to clear physical and spiritual space, while its essential oil is used to clear the head and quieten the mind for meditative practices.

Lavender: Wonderfully aromatic lavender has a protective quality whilst being gentle and soothing. I think of lavender as the mamma bear of the plant world. She's strong, beautiful and just wants to help us soothe and ease our hurt.

Rose: With her spiky thorns the rose is also associated with protection. Her flower is linked to ancestor work, love, beauty and feminine/goddess energy.

Cedar rose: These wooden roses are gifts of the female cones of the deodar cedar. They start off in a traditional cone shape, slowly disintegrating to release their wing-shaped seeds. At the end of the process, the cone is left looking like a wooden rose and falls to the ground. I like to use cedar roses as a nod to the use of cedar as a plant essence. Plant essences are an energetic medicine; in this modality, cedar is used to help us release the pain of the past and let go of what no longer serves.

Method:

Cut your chosen plant materials to length and tie the plants together to form a torso, leaving some plant material to fan out like a skirt. Choose some more plants and tie to the torso horizontally to form a cross shape; these will be your doll's arms. Make sure you tie it tightly, as the plants will shrink as they dry. You can add flowers into the torso or skirt area of the doll for decoration. If you have a rose or a cedar rose, securely tie this at the top of the doll to form a face. Once finished, leave the doll in a well-ventilated place out of direct sunlight to dry. You will know she is dry once she feels crunchy to the touch.

For use:

Once dry, your witch worry doll is ready to go! You can either hold your doll and whisper your worries to her, or you can briefly write out what you wish to release on small slips of paper, roll them up and tuck them into the skirt of the doll. When you are ready to release these worries, pop your witch worry doll into a fireproof bowl and set her alight. Your worries and fears are being symbolically burned and released, to be transmuted into something more positive by the universe.

Once the doll has fully burned, mix the ashes with some water and cool any embers. Once it is safe to do so, return the ashes to the earth and give thanks for the energy exchange that took place.

HONOUR THY SELF

I would also suggest you create a space in your home that honours you and reminds you of how amazing and worthy of love you are. You could either create a vision board or an altar space.

Fill this space with images or statues that invoke feelings of love and joy, and remind you of your beautiful spirit. You can include flowers or plants, crystals, love notes from loved ones, photos of yourself. You could also include items that symbolise the type of business you wish to create, or the family you wish to have, as these are extensions of you and your energy. Make this space a celebration of you!

It is important that you have a candle in a safe space on this altar, or in the line of sight of the vision board. You can light this candle every day – the act of doing this daily will act as a trigger to your subconscious, creating a feedback loop that you are worthy of love and celebration. This is particularly important if you have struggled with self-love in the past.

Candles that are red, pink or white are best, as they are symbolically linked to love. You may also want to carve words like "love", "confidence", "joy", "self-esteem", "reverence", and "passion" onto the sides of the candle. Perhaps anoint the candle with a little olive oil mixed with rose essential oil, to seal your intentions in.

If you want this space to be extra potent, I suggest setting it up in front of a mirror. This will double the potency, because firstly, in seeing your reflection in the mirror as you visit this space each day, you can take the time to give yourself a smile and say some words of affirmation. Secondly, the mirror's reflective surface will reflect the altar space, essentially doubling the energetics of love and reverence out into the world around you.

It might also be nice to play music you love, to sing and dance to when you visit your self-love altar space. I love to listen to India Arie sing her incredible song "I Am Light" when I am in my space; it never fails to move me to tears and remind me how incredible we all are. Visit this space daily and make it a ritual experience; I find doing this in the morning as I get ready works best for me. Light your candle, perhaps burn some incense, play your music and spend some time looking at your reflection and appreciating all the goodness that is you. Sometimes it may be hard to find anything you like about yourself – that's okay, we've all been there. Take a moment and find little things to celebrate, such as appreciating that your body is healthy and functioning or giving thanks for your unbreakable spirit. On other days, you may feel like revelling in your beauty and uniqueness with words of gratitude. There is magic in feeling both ways, and this is your safe space to celebrate you, with no shame, no judgement, just love.

Mirror work is also something I've found invaluable. Louise Hay's positive affirmation work is helpful but I practise a slightly more confronting version. It involves a heart-to-heart sit down with yourself. If you have a mirror, set it up as suggested in your self-love altar space; this is the perfect spot to practise it.

MIRROR MIRROR

For this exercise, bring a comfy chair and set it up in front of a mirror. Make yourself a hot drink; a box of tissues and a journal to write your insights in may be good to have nearby. Sit down and pull your chair up to the mirror. Get comfortable and spend a few moments looking into your own eyes in the mirror. This in itself can feel very awkward and confronting. You can stop here and say some affirmations, or just sit gazing into your eyes if that feels intense. When you are ready, have a chat with yourself, just like you would with a close friend. Talk out all the problems you are having; be open and honest. Vent your frustrations and voice that inner critic you hear in your head. This critic is the voice that tells you that you aren't enough, you aren't loveable, and questions who you are to chase your dreams or show up the way you want in the world. During this practice, the most important thing is to maintain eye contact with yourself the whole time. Really focus on the light you see shining out of your own eyes; this is especially important when say anything mean or critical about yourself.

As you look into your own eyes, I want you to think of your reflection as a treasured friend, family member or your own child. Would you ever say these disparaging, critical things to these people? Would you be able to watch the light in their eyes dim, the sparkle disappear and the tears well up as you spoke harshly to them? I'm guessing you wouldn't, so why, my love, are you talking this way to yourself?

Give yourself time to process the emotions that are coming up. Be gentle with yourself. As you maintain eye contact with your reflection, I want you to tell yourself all the ways you matter, and all the wonderful qualities only you possess. Tell yourself you forgive yourself – for being over critical, for past mistakes, for whatever is coming up for you.

The Aftermath of Mirror Work

My mentor Erika Cramer once said, "Do you believe that the Divine makes mistakes?" I answered, "No, I don't believe the Divine makes mistakes." Erika then asked me why I thought I could tell the Divine they made a mistake with me. That hit me like a punch in the gut – who was I to treat any aspect of the Divine's creations with disgust or disdain? If I truly believed my own animist beliefs, how could I deny the Divine spark that was in me, and how could I not honour it?

When I did this mirror exercise for the first time after my divorce, I cried so much my head hurt. I looked into my eyes and, as I gave voice to my inner critic, I imagined they were the eyes of my daughters or my sons. I imagined one of my children thinking these thoughts about themselves. My heart broke at the thought of them thinking they were anything less than phenomenal, and at the idea of them not recognising their own magic when they looked in the mirror. Then my heart broke for myself, because I deserved that same fierce love from myself that I had been denying myself for decades.

I've done it several times since, and each time I feel another layer of self-loathing and self-criticism dissolve. Take it slow with this exercise and be willing to lean into the uncomfortable; our shadow self and our pain have so much wisdom to teach us. These aspects of ourselves are not the enemies; they are just our wounded teachers. If we show them compassion and acknowledge their presence within us, they will unlock a deeper level of wisdom, understanding and peace within us.

Annointing Yourself

Be gentle with yourself as insights and emotions come up. If you have access to a bathtub, I'd recommend a warm salt bath soak after you have finished your mirror exercise, to help energetically cleanse yourself.

If you don't have a bath, take a warm shower and envision the water running over you as a cleansing shower of light.

After you are cleansed, apply your body lotion or oil with love and reverence as you gently massage your body. Give thanks for your insights and send love to yourself. When I apply body oils or make-up, I like to bless each body part as I apply it. For example, as I rub body oil into my skin, I say: "Bless my body to give me the strength to carry me and my loved ones through the day". As I put on my eye cream, I say, "Bless my eyes, to see beauty and love." As I apply lipstick or lip balm, I say, "Bless my mouth, to speak wisdom, kindness and truth."

There are endless affirmations or blessings you could use as you anoint your skin with the products you use every day. It's a nice way to really bring you into the present moment and send some love to yourself whilst setting intentions.

Perhaps spend some time journaling your thoughts and then either indulge in a quiet night of self-care or have an early night of restorative sleep.

To add an extra layer to your self-love routine, you may like to use essential oils to help enhance your feelings of wellbeing, to increase energy levels or to bring about feelings of love and confidence. You can add five drops of your chosen essential oil to your aromatherapy diffuser or make your own body oil blend for self-massage.

Diffusing essential oils is great because it can set the mood in your household, whilst anointing your skin with essential oils in a body blend or adding some to your bath adds a feeling of luxury and reverence. If you wish to create a lasting scent with your essential oils, it's a good idea to have a blend of top, middle and base notes. Base notes linger the longest and are like the glue that holds the essential oil synergy (the combination of essential oil scents you have chosen) together. They are generally, but not always, the essential oils that come from woods and resins. Base notes tend to last for around a week. Middle notes tend to be herbaceous plants and flowers and will last a few days. Top notes will evaporate the fastest, over a few hours, and are generally the light citrus scents or essential oils from tree leaves like eucalyptus.

I believe less is more when it comes to essential oils, because they are very potent and it takes a lot of plant material to create a few millilitres, so I like to use them with respect.

A third dilution is my preferred ratio for body blends – take your total amount of carrier oil and divide by three to get your total of essential oil drops. For example, use 100 millilitres of carrier oil and 33 drops total of essential oil. If you add essential oils to your bath, only use a few drops and always add something like Epsom salts or a few tablespoons of milk to the water to help disburse the oils.

Please always do your own research into essential oils. Just because they are natural doesn't mean they aren't incredibly potent. Essential oils *are not* safe for all age ranges, health conditions or life stages. Research to check what medications or health conditions are contraindicated. Always clearly label any bottles of essential oil blends you may create, with a list of ingredients and the date made. Keep the bottles out of sunlight, and use dark bottles if you can. Patch test before use for sensitivities, never ingest, always dilute and keep out of reach of children.

EVERYDAY ESSENTIAL OILS

⚹ JOY ⚹

FEEL HAPPY AND
DELIGHTED

Sandalwood
Orange
Ylang Ylang
Bergamot
Pettigrain

⚹ LOVE ⚹

ENHANCE LOVE OF SELF
AND OTHERS

Rose
Rose Geranium
Jasmine
Ylang Ylang

⚹ ANXIETY ⚹

FEEL GROUNDED AND
REDUCE ANXIETY

Frankincence
Patchouli
Lavender
Geranium

⚹ FOCUS ⚹

IMPROVE CLARITY AND
CONCENTRATION

Rosemary
Basil
Lemon
Lemongrass
Cypress
Ginger

⚹ PEACE ⚹

PROMOTE FEELINGS
OF CALM

Frinkincence
Neroli
Jasmine
Juniper
Roman Chamomile

⚹ UPLIFT ⚹

CHASE AWAY LOW MOOD
AND IRRITABILITY

Grapefruit
Lemon
Orange
Basil
Cedarwood

HEALING WITH WATER

*"There must be quite a few things a hot bath
won't cure, but I don't know many of them."*
~ *Sylvia Plath* ~

Hydrotherapy has been practised for health since the dawn of time. Most of us enjoy frolicking in cool waters in the heat of summer or luxuriating in a warm tub on a cold winter's day. There's something about the element of water that makes us feel safe to be in our emotions, perhaps because of a primordial link to feeling safe in our mother's womb. Bathing at home can provide us the much-needed space to process emotions and receive downloads of inspiration and wisdom. There's something about being surrounded and held by water that allows us deep emotional release. Nothing compares to a good sob in the shower when I'm feeling beat down by the world. As the hot water cascades around me, I can sink to the shower floor and cry as loudly as I want. My tears mix with the falling water, and my cries are muffled by the shower's downpour. It feels damn good to drop my guard and release my pain and visualise it all flowing away down the drain. At some point I feel fully decompressed; this is when ideas and wisdom come pouring in thick and fast. The shower is my place to think, and I always have my best ideas when I'm in this place. I always end my showers by visualising the water as pure rainbow light, cleansing me before I step back into the everyday world.

To make your shower even more therapeutic, you can hang bunches of aromatic plants in your shower to give you a hit of aromatherapy. The steam from the hot water will help release the volatile oils in the plants' leaves – just be sure to replace your plant material regularly. Popping a few drops of essential oils onto a face cloth or sponge and placing it in the corner of your shower will have the same effect. You can have a look at the essential oil chart for ideas on oils or aromatic plants you could use.

Baths for me are more ritualistic. I tend to go for a soak when I feel unwell, run-down and need a big dose of relaxation. If I'm filling the tub, I'm going all in on my self-care. There are big fluffy towels, a headrest, candles, atmospheric music, a drink at hand and water that is just the right temperature. The bath is my time to be alone and undisturbed!

Baths are also a great opportunity to add a few extra items to the water you are bathing in. You can get very specific with the items you choose and make your bath into a ritual. For example, you can customise a bath for self-love, healing, purification, or drawing creativity or abundance your way.

Epsom salts are fantastic for sore, tired muscles. Whilst **pink Himalayan salts** are great for times when you feel physically or energetically heavy and want to draw out toxins. If your aim is to detox, set a timer for ten minutes and then hop out of the bath. If you stay in over ten minutes, you're going to reabsorb all the nasties that the salt has drawn out of your body.

Essential oils are great to add in, but remember to add a few tablespoons of milk, milk powder, Castile soap or vegetable oil to help the essential oils disperse as they are not water soluble. Take care as the vegetable oil or Castile soap may make the bath slippery.

Crystals can also be added to the bath water. However, do be careful as not all crystals are suitable for use in water. Some crystals are soft and water will slowly dissolve them, and some crystals release toxins in water, so do your research. Crystals may also scratch or create chips on the surface of your bath or poke into skin, which isn't ideal either! I tend to only use smooth tumble stones of clear quartz or rose quartz in my bath water. Any other crystals I wish to invite into my bath energetically are kept up on a windowsill or bath ledge, well away from the water.

Plants also make a lovely addition to your bath and can be chosen for your intention or for their healing properties. For ease of clean up, place your plant materials in a large muslin bag, like a giant tea bag, and then place into the bath water. You could also seep the plants for 10–15 minutes in a tea pot, strain and add to the bath water. Again, do your own research for safety, allergies and contraindications. Please also remember that hot and cold water can alter blood pressure so exercise caution if you are pregnant or have blood pressure issues.

Some suggestions for plants to incorporate into your bath are:

Rose Petals: For self-love, romance, healing a broken heart, honouring the goddess. Rose water is rich in antioxidants, and could also be added in for its skin-soothing properties. I have found rose to be a potent ally in healing after heartbreak as she helps you get in touch with all facets of the feminine, both in physical and spiritual form. She is wisdom, sensuality, softness, strength and fierce protectiveness all in one.

Oats/Oat straw: Oats are full of protein, saponins, vitamins and minerals and are particularly soothing for itchy skin conditions such as eczema. Oats/oat straw are also linked to money, fertility and abundance.

Lavender: Great for bringing anxiety relief and peace to a busy, frazzled mind. Lavender is also deeply mothering and protective, so she's a good one to add into your bath when you're in need of rest and respite. Lavender is also anti-inflammatory and anti-fungal, soothing to minor skin injuries and is a great addition to the bath if you have a headache or other aches and pains. Lavender is also ideal if you wish to have a good sleep or do some dream work.

Chamomile: The flowers of chamomile look like little suns, with white rays extending from a large yellow disc. It is the perfect addition to baths when you are in need of mental relaxation and soothing. It is also very calming to itchy skin conditions. Chamomile helps reduce inflammation and is antimicrobial. Magically, chamomile corresponds with protection and purification, so it is a good one to bathe in before any ritual work, before meditation or even before big important events.

Mint: Mint is the perfect addition to a bath on a hot summer day, as its cooling and refreshing properties are hugely welcome! Mint can also wake up and re-energise you, so it's best to use mint when you want to be alert. Mint is also great for drawing wealth and abundance to you and works to enhance vitality and energy.

Orange blossoms/Neroli: Who doesn't love the scent of orange blossoms? The aroma puts you straight into a relaxed, happy state and there is always an abundance of blossoms on the trees so you can add the little white flowers to your bath without fear of reducing your orange harvest. Orange blossom is stress-reducing for the mind and decongesting for the skin, as well as being anti-inflammatory and antimicrobial. Magically, it corresponds with love, luck and money.

Jasmine: One of my favourite scents, the star-shaped flowers of jasmine invoke a feeling of sensuality, joy and relaxed openness. Sprinkle through your bath if you wish to work with the energies of love and sensuality or to enhance psychic dreams and visions.

Eucalyptus leaf: The freshly scented eucalyptus leaf is a good one to bathe with if you are feeling run down and need to boost your mental state, as well as your immune system. Adding eucalyptus to your bath can also add to the water's warming and relaxing properties. Eucalyptus has been associated with healing, cleansing and removing negative energies.

Tea tree: Tea tree is a fabulous, healing plant medicine. It is antiseptic, anti-fungal and anti-inflammatory. It is great for cuts, abrasions, acne and helping to soothe and heal skin. Similarly to eucalyptus, tea tree is associated with protection, purification and clearing negative energies on all levels – physical, mental, emotional and spiritual – so it's a brilliant additive to your bath when you are feeling drained and fatigued with psychic or emotional gunk. If you live in New Zealand, Mānuka and Kānuka have very similar properties, so you could use sprigs of these trees instead. Kānuka has a gentler energy to it, so it is better suited if you feel you need a softer approach.

WATER WISDOM

Water has the ability to keep us hydrated and to cleanse our bodies and our soul. Water teaches us about sheer power and energetic force through its raging rivers and spectacular waterfalls. Water cleanses us, renews us and soothes us with the music of gently babbling brooks or the tinkling of water splashing in a fountain.

Water also has the ability to hold memory. Japanese scientist and pioneer of water research Dr Masaru Emoto has shown us that our thoughts and intentions can change physical properties. Because of this ability, water has long been prayed over and used in blessings, baptisms and healings by many cultures. From sacred wells, to rivers, lakes and springs, water has been revered throughout human history. I'd be willing to bet that if you looked deep enough into the history of the region you currently live in, there would be a sacred body of water or a river or lake with a mythological story attached to it.

In his work, Masaru Emoto conducted experiments on water molecules.[6] Specifically, he claimed his experiments showed that words, prayer, music and even intentions could physically alter the molecular structure of water. These experiments resulted in the formation of beautiful water crystals when exposed to positive words, intentions, and prayer, and malformed crystals when water is exposed to disharmonious music or negative or harsh wording.[7]

Because water has been so important to many cultures across time and space, I think that there is wisdom in treating water with reverence. I often pray and bless the water I bathe or shower in, or as I cook food or prepare something to drink. In my home, I have stickers with sacred geometry and positive words like "wisdom", "love", and "abundance" stuck on the water chamber of the coffee machine and onto the electric kettle.

I often write words of positivity discretely in marker onto the bottom of water bottles, and I encourage my children to do the same. You could also use water bottles with crystal chambers or place your water bottles atop coloured squares of paper to infuse with the energy of a specific colour.

Even if there was absolutely nothing to this theory of water holding energy, these practices still become acts of mindfulness and gratitude, a way to infuse the day with a little magic.

The idea of water holding memory is also partially behind the theory of homeopathic medicine, Bach flower remedies and plant or crystal essences. These modalities rely on water holding an energetic imprint or memory of a specific substance or plant to create an energetic remedy that will work to help bring our own spirit and energetics back into alignment. As such, this can often bring comfort to our physical bodies too.

Author and Bach flower practitioner Mechthild Scheffer explains that, "the Bach Flower acts as a catalyst, reconnecting the specific, blocked contact between the Soul and the personality. The Soul can be heard again by the personality. Where there was disharmony and rigidity, life flows again."[8]

I love to use flower essences for myself, my children and even my dogs, in times when emotions are frayed and we need a little bit more support. I use a combination of traditional Bach Flower essences and my own homemade flower and crystal essences. I have found them to be really effective for emotional support. In fact, I made my own throat chakra remedy to help me find my voice, and took it every time I sat down to write this book!

You can make your own energetic essence easily at home, as you only need a few key ingredients and the ability to look at a flower, plant or crystal and understand what each has to offer in the way of energetic support. It is also important to note that you *do not* use any plants or flowers that have been *sprayed, collected by a roadside or are toxic or poisonous in any way*. The same goes with crystals you chose to use. I myself will only use clear quartz or rose quartz. Please research, as not all crystals are suitable to be submerged in water and some crystals will also leech toxins into the water. *Always do your own thorough research!*

~ MAKE YOUR OWN ~ FLOWER ESSENCE

To make your own flower/plant essence simply wait for a sunny day. First thing in the morning, fill a glass bowl with around a cup or two of pure spring water.

Go outside and find the most beautiful, perfect flower or plant specimen (that you have identified as safe for human consumption). For an example, let's pretend we are making a rose flower essence. Find the most perfect roses and give it a gentle shake (to make sure there are no bugs!)

- Carefully snip the flowers so they fall into the bowl of water without it touching your hands. Cover the surface of the water in roses.

- Place the bowl of water out of the way of any pets or children and allow it to sit and infuse, undisturbed for several hours in the full sun without any shadows crossing the bowl.

- After 3□4 hours bring the bowl inside and strain off the water from the rose.

- Fill a clean, sterilised, dark bottle, half way up with brandy (that is 80-proof alcohol) –the brandy acts as a preservative for the flower essence.

- Top the bottle up with your rose essence water. Put a lid on and gently shake to combine.

- Label with the date and the type of flower essence you have made. This is now your "Mother" essence. Store in a dark place.

Your mother essence is to be diluted and never consumed directly. So the next step is to create a "stock" bottle.

- Fill a sterilised 30ml bottle with brandy. Add 2 drops of your Mother essence. Clearly label your bottle, 'rose essence stock bottle'; date. It is from this bottle you will create your future flower remedies.

- In order to use your stock flower essence you must again, dilute it. You can do this by filling a small clean, sterilised 15 ml dropper bottle with 10 mls of spring water and 5 mls of brandy. Add two drops of your flower essence stock bottle, if you had multiple different flower essences and you wanted to make a custom essence mixture you could add up to five different flower essences (so 10 drops total).

- Clearly label your ingredients e.g.; 10ml water, 5ml brandy, 2 drops rose flower essence and the date you made it. This is now your flower essence medicine. From this flower essence medicine bottle, take two drops of mixture under the tongue, or pop 2 drops into a glass of water, up to four times a day, as needed.

You can follow this method with your chosen (correctly identified, safe for human consumption) leaves, flowers or crystals so you can make a variety of essences for your needs. You could also place the spring water in a quartz singing bowl and play it, to infuse it with a particular chakra-balancing energy.

Once bottled and labelled, you might like to increase your essence's energetics by placing it in a crystal grid for a day or so. The rose essence could be included in a crystal grid of rose quartz to further strengthen the energetics of love and compassion.

Another idea would be to use spring water that has been left out to infuse under a full moon or a particular moon phase that has the energies you desire to harness.

CHAPTER 10

ANCESTORS

*"I was born by myself but carry the spirit and blood of
my father, mother and my ancestors. So I am really
never alone. My identity is through that line."*

~ Ziggy Marley ~

We don't often stop to think about those who have come before us – the people and personalities who make up our lineage, whose genetic material resides in our bodies. I'm not sure we actually think of them as actual human beings, with their own hopes and dreams. But rather, we see them instead as figures that occupied a role: mother, father, grandparent, great aunt. It boggles my mind to think of all the moments, the synchronicities, the decisions that had to happen, in order for our parents to meet and for us to birthed, let alone all that had to align for our grandparents, our great grandparents and so on to meet.

Everything that had to happen historically just for us to be born is nothing short of miraculous.

Even the very earth we walk on is made up of the dead; the fertility and quality of life within our soil is dependent on the bodies of our plant, animal and human kin returning to the earth when our physical selves cease working and our souls depart. This nourishes new life into existence. Long-dead stars light our skies. Our ancestors' gifts of immunity, genetics and traits are passed on through the generations. Death influences our physical existence more than we care to acknowledge.

The dead need us too – without us, they would have no one to honour them, to tell fond stories or cautionary tales, to speak them into the land of the living and draw upon lessons they learned or taught us. Working with ancestors is a symbiotic relationship, beneficial to both us and them.

Ancestor work can really be beneficial when it comes to the development of self, when we wish to heal old traumas and move past old, ingrained patterning. I believe when we do this, we are not only healing ourselves, but also releasing the traumas and stuck patterning that may be in our lineage. A mentor of mine suggested that in order for us to overcome our critical voices and step into a new version of ourselves, it is beneficial to create an alter ego. We can create an imagined version of ourselves that encompasses all the positive qualities we wish to attain, while we work on ourselves to get there.

While I like this idea, I'm not great at acting or imagining a different version of myself, especially when I am continually faced with my shortcomings every time I step into a new or uncomfortable situation. The suggestion certainly got me thinking, so I had to think of a new way to step outside of myself and call in traits and talents that felt not so easily available to me. This is where ancestor work really came into play.

Some research shows that when a person goes through hardships and times of great stress, such as war, famine, or great trauma, these events become encoded into their DNA. Research on animals and humans alike has shown that the impact of traumatic events experienced by the mother in turn affects early offspring development. Further research is also discovering that this trauma will actually be encoded into the DNA of subsequent generations.[9] Think about the impact this could potentially have on us. If, generations ago, your ancestors lived through a period of famine, this cellular memory could potentially show up in your life today. You could have a troubling relationship with food or feel the need to hoard and accumulate resources and wealth. This could even emerge as that gnawing, empty feeling inside that makes you look for external objects such as new shoes or clothes to fill that hole in you the feeling creates. Imagine how much more insight and compassion you would have for yourself if you could see and understand these cellular threads.

With this in mind, it would stand to reason that positive traits such as resilience, power, and empathy, as well as skills from lessons learned and lives lived, would also be encoded into our DNA and passed on.

The blood that flows through our veins carries a wealth of information from our ancestors that we can tap into – we already contain what we need. When I need confidence, self-belief and the ability to take up space, instead of turning to an alter ego, I draw upon the power that is already inside me, gifted to me by my ancestors. I imagine them, and it is their strength I call upon.

Not all of us are familiar with our ancestry. History and stories can be lost along the way, with migration to new countries, scandals, family disputes and the passing of time. If this is the case for you, it could be beneficial to spend some time researching your lineage.

Perhaps you could start by researching and asking family for stories about what your great grandparents were like, what hardships they faced, how they survived and how they thrived. It is helpful to trace as far back as you can.

If you cannot readily find information on family members, turn your attention instead to researching time periods and places you know your ancestors lived. You could research the hardships faced by people from those countries and eras. Look into the history of your surname, which can give you a wealth of information on family creeds, clan or tribal history, typical locations these families lived, as well as occupations. From this information, you can then create a picture of traits your ancestors would have likely developed. You can then create a list of traits you would like to focus on calling in for your self-development and wellbeing.

It may also be helpful to create a list of shadow traits or negative aspects that may have been passed on as well. This way you can be mindful of what healing work may need to be done.

Researching the culture and spiritual practices of your lineage can also help you to feel grounded and connected. I am currently immersed in Celtic Studies, and it has given me a new depth of connectedness and peace I have never felt before. In understanding the early beliefs of my ancestors, their connection and reverence for the land, I can see my own animist beliefs reflected back at me through time. I can see how these beliefs are so similar to many other indigenous cultures, which helps me to feel further threads of connection, understanding and respect. This in turn helps me to understand my place in the world and how to work with the Spirit of the land on which I currently reside.

For example, this is how working with ancestors has helped me.

My nervous system seems to be wired with a tendency towards anxiety. I am also highly sensitive and experienced years of low self-confidence – my biggest demon has always been self-worth. After the divorce, I felt shame and a sense of failure at being a single mother. As I began healing myself, I realised that I had reached a point that my maternal line probably longed for.

I was a solo mum, with four incredible children, my own home and my own income stream. My extended family were supportive of me and I lived in a society that didn't shun single parents. I was living life on my own terms; my current reality was probably the future my great-grandmothers could only dream about. While I pondered my maternal line, I realised that if I was hurting or feeling overwhelmed, I could draw on the strength I already had in my DNA.

I've been told that my great-great-great-grandma was the village seer back in Scotland. Other women in my family have the gift of reoccurring prophetic dreams. These women help me to embrace my "witchy" side when the memories of witch trials and shame for being different is still very much alive in the collective consciousness. This connection helps me to have the courage to show up in all my spiritual glory!

My great-grandma had the strength and determination to pack up her family, board a ship and sail the lengthy and unpleasant journey from

Scotland to New Zealand in search of a better future. In New Zealand, she birthed and lost two sons in their early childhood years; despite the heartbreak she experienced, she showed extraordinary resilience in raising her two surviving daughters. Of course I can draw on that strength and fortitude to rebuild a new life for myself after divorce! Further inspiration came from my clan's motto, "Royal is my race". When I first heard it, I thought it was very pretentious; however, nowadays it reminds me to straighten my crown and show up when I feel small and unworthy. Who was I to play small? Who was I to not try and live my best life, when I was the accumulation of all my ancestors' hopes, dreams, hardships and battles?

The strength of my ancestors is my inspiration and my motivation as I move forward through hard times in life. They are the key to understanding some of my shadow aspects; they keep me rooted and grounded.

HONOURING YOUR ANCESTORS

Setting up a space in your home to honour your ancestors and bring them into your daily life is something that I would highly recommend. It could be as simple as hanging some photos or portraits on a wall, or it could be a dedicated altar space that you deck out especially for your ancestors. If you choose to create an altar space, be sure to include memorabilia, such as clan tartans, antiques, letters, or keepsakes handed down through the generations, as well as some offerings such as a bowl of salt, flowers, tobacco, incense, alcohol, coffee and the like.

I don't like to mix photos of the living with the dead on the altar, so I have photos of my ancestors on my altar and then have photos of my children on the wall above the altar, like a visual family tree. Some people prefer not to mix photos of the living with the dead, but it's all personal preference.

A plant offering that I find works quite well on an ancestral altar is a Rose of Jericho. This is one of the most brilliant houseplants out there. It is so easy to care for because it can dry out completely and "come back to life", and unfurls when placed in a small amount of water. Because of its ability to spend long periods of time without water (it simply closes up into a ball and looks like a tumble weed), this plant is often kept in families and handed down through generations. To me, this makes it the perfect plant link for the ancestral altar. When I am working with the ancestors and asking for help in a specific area, I fill a shallow bowl with water and place my Rose of Jericho in it, so that it opens up and unfolds. Once I'm done, I allow it to dry back up again. I hope that if I care for this plant well enough, it will be handed down to one of my children so they can use it on their altar space.

Other common offerings for your ancestral altar are candles, as they are lovely to light in remembrance each day, and foods that relatives liked to eat. Roses are a wonderful offering, because their history has long been intertwined with human history. Roses were one of the first plants humans built a relationship with and started to cultivate for use.

I find food for altars a bit tricky as I don't want to attract insects. I also have two dogs who would help themselves to food if it was left out! To get around this, I use plates of dried spices or fruit (which I throw away before it rots) and I also use an offering bottle. This bottle combines the traditional libation of alcohol with spices and herbs that have specific meaning. I put it in a pretty bottle, and this stays on my altar as a permanent "food" offering for my ancestors.

~ OFFERING BOTTLE ~

Find a pretty glass bottle with a stopper. Fill the bottle with the following:

- Dried fruit, I used pear which symbolises wisdom and health; you could use apple for knowledge.
- Cinnamon quills for good fortune
- Lavender for peace
- Rose and cardamon for love
- Juniper berries for luck and protection
- Rosemary for remembrance
- Calendula for warmth and communication
- Citrus peel for happiness and joy

Instructions:

1. Fill the bottle to the top with a favourite alcohol, then put the stopper in and seal with wax. You can then keep this offering bottle on your altar without worry of ants or pets getting into it!

~ ANCESTOR WREATH ~

1. You might also like to try your hand at weaving a remembrance wreath for your altar space. This is a great way to fuse your focus and intent whilst expressing yourself creatively. Weaving is relatively simple, although if you are skilled at weaving I'm sure you could create something amazingly complex if you so desire. All you need is some plant materials to weave with; grapevines, willow, and wisteria vine are usually relatively easy to find locally and grow rampantly enough to be able to cut lengths that suit the size of the wreath you wish to make. Some string or coloured thread and some photos or small trinkets of loved ones.

2. Firstly, cut your vines to the length of the circle you wish to create. If you harvest the plants yourself, be sure to leave an offering at the base of the plant as thanks.

3. Fashion a few of the vines or willow into a rough circle. You can tie a piece of string or twist some wire to keep the circle secure. Then, set about weaving the rest of the vines in and out of the circle until your wreath is shaped the way you like it. I like to also weave in a few sprigs of rosemary for remembrance.

4. Weave your string, ribbon or thread around the wreath you have fashioned and also across the middle, inner circle of the wreath, so you create a spider web effect in the middle. Be sure to keep the thread nice and tight, as your plant material will shrink as it dries. This thread symbolises the threads of fate and also the thread of connection that ties us all together; it's also going to be where you attach your trinkets and photos.

5. When you are happy with the wreath you have created, you can then attach your small trinkets or photos to the strings in the middle of the wreath. You could attach them with small pegs, wire or even paper clips.

6. Hang your wreath up on the wall above your altar and it will dry over time. If you find your thread has become loose as the material dries, you can either re-wrap it to tighten or do as I do and tuck crystals, feathers or dried flowers under the loose thread to bulk it out a bit a more and add interest.

When working with your ancestors, it is worth remembering that as in life, not all the people in our blood line were sweetness and light. There will be ancestors who created trauma for themselves and inflicted it, sometimes willingly, on others. There is always shadow mixed with the light. When we choose to work on healing ourselves and we actively ask our ancestors along for the ride, we start to undo those knots of pain and trauma. We release stuck patterning within our bloodline. When we heal, we are healing the generations that came before us and will come after us.

EXERCISE

If you would like to connect more to your ancestors, I would suggest the following:

- Research what your family or your culture do to honour and connect with the dead. Are there specific holidays, feast days or rituals that are important? How could you replicate these in your own life?
- Are there specific plants or foods that have cultural ties to ancestor veneration that you could incorporate into your rituals?

- Do you have room in your house to set up an ancestral altar space? If so, what objects would you like to incorporate into this space? Do you have trinkets, photos, or offerings you would like to use?

- If you don't have room for an altar space, could you set up a photo wall of family members, framed family memorabilia, or even a framed copy of your family tree?

- If you don't know much about your family history, could you take an ancestry DNA test to give you more insight into where to focus your research.

- Look into myths and folktales that link to your family's culture or to the lands your ancestors came from. Often these stories are rich in symbolism that can give you more insight to the beliefs, landscapes and the way of life your ancestors lived. Armed with this information, you can then create rituals and practices to connect with your ancestors.

- I like to have a tarot deck and an oracle deck that I only use for ancestor work. If this appeals to you, have a look around to see what decks may be appropriate for you.

- Dig deep enough and you will always find trauma and sadness in your lineage. Perhaps you are already acutely aware of this. People make mistakes; some people are hugely misguided during their lifetime. Famine, war, discrimination, colonisation, and violence can make up a part of what our ancestors experienced or inflicted on others. If you are aware of such things happening, it can be hard to reconcile this and connect with your ancestors. If this is the case, you may wish to look for ways to facilitate healing, or at the very least forgiveness and understanding, in a way that feels appropriate and applicable to you. Keep in mind that this can be heavy work and it is okay to take it slow or ask others for help and support. Your personal spiritual beliefs may also help bring you solace; for example, I believe that jealousy, greed, violence and bigotry are very human-based and that once someone passes on to Spirit they gain a bigger perspective and understanding that helps them to make amends and heal.

CHAPTER 11

RITUALS TO LIVE BY

*"We are part of the great energetic weave of
the earth. Each time we participate in our
own weaving, we affect the whole."*
~ Amantha Murphy[10] ~

We are gifted with time and seasons here on this earth. For some of us the time is short, over in a season or two. Others get to experience many seasons, and time seems to stretch on forever. It's easy to get caught up in the to-do lists of life, rushing to carry out activities and work that needs to be done. We forget to pause and relish the moments we are in. We wonder why we burn out, why illness suddenly seems to hit us, why stress and anxiety seem to be our constant companions. We give so much thought to what others may think of us if we drop the ball, let someone down, or if we say no to doing something we really don't want to do. We forget to tune into ourselves.

We are cyclical beings, and we see this reflected in the rhythms of our natural world too: the ebb and flow of the tides, the waxing and waning of the moon, the seasons of sunshine and lush growth, and seasons of cold and hibernation. Nature isn't all growth and activity all the time, so why do we expect constant production and energetic output from ourselves?

It's important to spend time going within, to honour the periods in life when we need quiet surrender and time alone, just as much as we honour and celebrate the times of vitality, creativity and production. There are immense gifts in honouring the cycles we find ourselves in − even the hard ones. Especially the hard ones. No one can tell you the correct amount of time to grieve, or how to adequately voice your anger or your fear. These are the emotions and situations we tend to hide or try to rush through, in an effort to push the pain away and be back to "normal", and then we miss part of the healing. A bit of that thorn snaps off in our rush and that part stays embedded in us, forever a tender part of our body and soul. It remains a pain point that we fiercely protect, that may cause us to lash out when we don't mean to. What if we honoured this part of ourselves instead?

How different would we be if we processed our pain, if we celebrated, nurtured and created rituals to honour the hard knocks in our life? Death, divorce and traumatic events shape us in ways we don't always have the words for, but in creating a ritual or gifting ourselves the time we need to retreat and heal, it can help us find words to acknowledge the gifts and find the wisdom we need to process and adapt.

THE POWER OF RITUAL

We used to have rituals and celebrations that honoured all seasons and all parts of our life; I believe it's essential to bring this practice back. Look around and research for inspiration, and then create your own rituals to celebrate and honour your life – the fantastic, joyful milestones and the heartbreaking, earth-shattering ones. These are the events that shape you and, as such, should be acknowledged and marked in some way. You can do this alone if it feels right, or gather like-minded souls to help you mark this passage in time.

During my separation period, I was grieving the loss of my husband who, though alive, was lost to me. I was having a hard time trying to honour the pain of my loss. After all, it was the relationship that was dead and not the person. I felt ashamed for feeling the intense grief and bereavement I didn't think I had any right to. My wonderful friend came around and created a ritual for me. We sat outside and we wove threads of cord around my hands. I visualised myself letting the cords of attachment go as he cut the cords for me. We dug a hole under an apple tree, placed the cords in the hole and we then overlaid the cord with a crystal grid. I whispered words of relief as we covered the cord and crystals over with the soft earth; it was the symbolic funeral I had no idea I needed. My friend knew, and that day he gave me such a gift. He saw me, honoured me and allowed me a way to see and honour myself too. I was able to start to let go and move on after that day – such is the power of ritual.

As humans we quite naturally crave a ritualised life. Ritual brings us comfort and safety and a certain sense of stability in amongst all of the incontrollable events and experiences.

Think about this; how often do you brew a cup of tea or coffee and reach for your favourite mug? Or do you have a morning routine that you follow in the same order every morning to get ready for the day? These examples are rituals at their most basic level: a group of actions performed in a prescribed order.

As much as we crave ritual for comfort and stability, we also draw on rituals to set apart certain experiences as out of the ordinary or special.

Think along the lines of a wedding celebration, or a funeral, or important religious feast/celebration days. Many cultures worldwide celebrated the equinox and solstices to mark the changing of seasons and passage of time. The seasons as well as the waxing and waning of the moon all naturally invite us to honour our own cyclical nature; and the ebb and flow of our energies. Ritual has always been linked to both the light and the dark. The celebration of the light found in life through comfort, joy, food, song and dance; and the celebration of the dark, with celebrations to honour the dying, death and the ending of cycles.

In creating our own rituals we are actively tuning into the divine and we are also acknowledging, honouring and validating our experiences; we also initiate ourselves into a wider, collective experience. This initiation allows us to move from focusing just on "me" to seeing the wider threads of connection of our kin (human, animal, nature) both past and present. Ritual has this unique way of both honouring our individual selves whilst also moving us into recognising and connecting with the wider world. There is huge medicine in doing this, creating a ritual that is meaningful to our own experiences and way of living becomes not only a form of reverence, but also a way to tune into the rhythms of life around us.

Ritual is important for both the big and the small moments of our lives. Transitional, liminal times particularly benefit from the creation of ritual. Examples of such times are: moving from child to adult, conception/moving into motherhood, relationship endings, moving house, new business ventures, children leaving home/empty nest, menopause and the list goes on.

There are many brilliant books on creating rituals for both big and small events, a quick look in a metaphysical store or an online bookshop will turn up a treasure trove of authors to learn from!

I will share with you a few rituals I have found helpful in my own journey, in the hopes that it will spark some inspiration to create your own personalised rituals.

RITUALS FOR DAILY LIFE

I have outlined a lot of the rituals I use for creating sacred space, self-love and self-care in the previous pages. But there is one ritual I never fail to do and that is my morning ritual. I go to my altar space, light my abundance candle, apply a blessing water and say a prayer for the day and pull a card for guidance. It's simple and it grounds me into the present moment, preparing me for the day ahead.

In addition to this, I also create my own celebrations for the winter and summer solstice and spring and autumn equinox to honour the cycles of nature and to focus in on the gifts of each season. For example, on the summer solstice I make flower crowns and focus on all the abundance and vitality in my life, whereas the winter solstice invites me to create a cosy space, light candles and focus on tending to my inner world and healing. The autumn equinox energy brings me deep peace and gratitude and allows me to tune into and connect with my ancestors; whilst the spring equinox offers me the opportunity to usher in fresh new energies and perspectives after a season of rest and taking it slow.

New moons are also my monthly touch point; the new moon is all about setting intentions, creating and building momentum. It's a really hopeful energy which I enjoy (more so than the full moon which I find very draining) so each new moon I do a full tarot spread for myself and focus in on what I wish to create for the month ahead. I will often write down any special or big projects I want to bring into fruition and then bury the paper under the soil of a potted plant or a seedling. As I water and care for that plant I visualise my project being nurtured and growing too. If you would like to learn more about working with moon phases there are many books, almanacs and apps for your phone that will help you to learn more and track the phases of the moon.

I would highly recommend that you spend time looking back at old journals, tracking your bleed or hormonal cycle (men also have their own ebbs and flow of hormones), paying attention to moon phases and seasons to see how they affect you. Where I find the full moon draining, you may find it invigorating and the perfect time to get in touch with your intuition and inner power. Once armed with this knowledge you will be better able to create rituals to nurture and honour yourself.

RITUAL FOR SIGNIFICANT EVENTS

Whilst it's not unusual for us in western society to celebrate birthdays and weddings with specific rituals, we don't usually have rituals in this day and age for events such as coming of age/first bleed, moving house, divorce/relationship endings or beginning the path of healing a specific trauma. These transitional moments, when we leave a life phase, or path behind are pivotal points in our lives and deserve to be acknowledged and honoured. The following are some ideas that you may like to use or adapt to your own needs.

Moon Box

Our daughters' first menstrual bleeds are something to celebrate, a coming of age moment which signals that many fertile years (physically and metaphorically) are ahead. In our collective history, menstruation has been both honoured and also vilified — made shameful and "dirty". Reclaiming a girls first menstruation as a way to celebrate her entry into womanhood is incredibly beautiful for both mother/parent and daughter.

As my two daughters got closer to the age they would begin to bleed, I created a moon box to gift them on the day of their first bleed. I bought a large, pretty box and into it I placed all the items I thought would be helpful for a young woman. Practical sanitary items as well as items that encouraged using menstruation as a monthly invitation to reflect and tap into intuition. My aim was to create a box that would make my daughters feel pampered, empowered and honoured.

You could use the following list and/or add to it.
- Sanitary items — I included a mixture of products for my daughters to sample as well as period panties
- A cute little pouch/bag to keep sanitary products in for school
- Heat pack and homeopathic remedies for period cramps
- Herbal teas
- A journal and a pack of oracle cards to encourage self-reflection and tuning into intuition
- A few rose quartz crystals for self-love
- An essential oil massage blend for balancing hormones and reducing period pain
- An eye mask for napping

- A special piece of jewellery (I choose moon phase pendants)
- A book about menstruation and body changes – I really like *Reaching for the Moon* by Lucy H. Pearce

You might like to gift this to your daughter and create a special ritual, take her out for a meal with other women or simply spend the day with her for some quality 1:1 time.

Although I have focused on the importance of celebrating our daughters' first bleed, it is important to honour our sons' coming of age too. Perhaps you could create a box filled with items that would be appropriate for your son and his needs and gift that to him when he first starts shaving his facial hair or at some such time that you feel signals he is moving into manhood and create a ritual to honour him. The same goes for if your child identifies as non-binary or gender fluid. Use these ideas to create a box and an experience that celebrates and honours them.

Coming of age rituals used to be celebrated in many cultures and they create a safe space that allows for your child to transition into young adulthood, knowing they are supported and can seek guidance without fear or shame. This transitionary space also encourages the movement from focusing in on "me" to seeking connections with the wider community and a shift into focusing on the collective or "we".

MOVING

I have read that moving house is one of the top three most stressful events you can encounter in your life, apparently its right up there with death and divorce! I'm not sure whether it's because I moved so much in my childhood or whether it's just that I love creating sacred spaces, but I actually enjoy the process of setting up a whole new space to work and live in.

If you are like me and become quite attached to the home and land you live on, you might like to craft a ritual to thank the property for housing you and your family and looking after you on your journey. Perhaps you could offer the land some new plantings, or leave food out for the local land spirit (and wild life that may frequent your property), or perhaps you could simply bury a heartfelt prayer of gratitude and a few crystals as an offering.

After the house is emptied out of your belongings, I would recommend you thoroughly cleanse the space with a spiritual water floor wash and perhaps saining the space so the energy is clear for the new occupants. I would also carry out this process at your new property too. Cleanse the space before you move in to remove the previous owners' energy and also make an offering on your land to "introduce" yourself to its energies when you move in. You might even like to bury crystals at certain points on your new property, creating a kind of crystal grid to invite prosperity, love or protection, or plant certain herbs or trees that symbolise the type of energy you wish to invite into your new home.

DIVORCE/ENDING OF RELATIONSHIPS

It's hard to let relationships go, even when you know it's for the best it can be a messy and painful process. Any relationship, whether positive or negative will have had an impact on you. Lessons are learned, growth comes through relationship, treasured memories are created. Heart opening (or closing) experiences and perhaps homes, businesses or children may have also been created from your union. Dissolution is hard and often we are expected to dust ourselves off, move on and get back out into the dating game as if nothing has ever happened.

I believe it's healthy to take time to grieve the loss of the relationship, to mourn what could have been, heal any trauma and shore up any gaps in our self-love game before jumping back into the dating pool. It can be all too tempting to distract oneself from pain and loss with a new (or a string) of relationships.

A ritual created just for you can help you to honour the ending and cut the ties that once bound you to another. If you are into working with the moon, then this ritual could be done during the waning moon phase (this occurs between a full and new moon) and it is the best phase for releasing, banishing and letting go of what no longer serves you.

Preform this ritual just before sunset, so that you can visualise the sun setting on the old relationship. Depending on the break up you had, you may want to photograph this sunset so you have a visual reminder of this release that you can anchor into when you need it.

Find two sticks of similar lengths (to symbolise you and your ex). You might like to choose sticks from trees that have particular symbolism (apple for love and relationships, pine for prayers and healing etc) and loosely wrap a length of white cord around both sticks, be sure to leave a little slack as you wrap the cord as you want to be able to cut the sticks apart. This cord symbolises the connection you had in your relationship. White symbolises a fresh start or a clean slate as well as purity of spirit.

Spend some time in meditation holding the wrapped sticks. Give thanks for what you have learned, any good or growth that came from the relationship etc. Then move on to visualising any hurt you have being healed and the ties that connected yourself and your significant other dissolving. Perhaps imagine yourself cocooned in a protective healing light, or you could envision being wrapped in a shiny reflective surface if your ex is being malicious. This surface will bounce off and reflect all the ill will back to the ex who is sending the toxic energy your way. Visualise your life ahead of you, filled with opportunities, new people and wonderful experiences coming your way. See yourself as happy, whole and healed. When you are ready open your eyes take a few breaths to centre and cut the cord that ties the two sticks together.

Bury these two sticks and their cords in two separate holes. You could put protective crystals such as obsidian, black tourmaline or even black kyanite (to help severe cords) in the hole with the stick that symbolised your ex, alongside white flower petals, or sprigs of olive leaves to symbolise peace. In the hole in which you place the stick that symbolises you, place crystals associated with energies you wish to draw to you. Citrine for happiness and abundance, amethyst for spiritual growth, rose quartz for self-love, clear quartz for clarity and amplifying your own personal power etc. Place in flowers or herbs that symbolise love, luck etc.

Cover the holes up and thank the earth for receiving and holding space for your ritual. Watch the sun go down, snap a photo to remind you, that this is the day you said goodbye to the past and welcomed in fresh new energies. Spend the rest of the evening doing something beautiful just for you. Eat a good meal, have a bath, hang out with friends, whatever fills your cup up.

The beauty of creating your own rituals is that it allows you to bring reverence and the mystical into your everyday life. You can create rituals that are solely for you or you could create ones that allow you to invite friends and family to participate. Your rituals can be heavy on symbology and ceremony, or paired down and simple, some may not look very different from how you conduct your daily life, all are equally potent and beautiful.

You may like to spend a little time journaling on how you would like to incorporate ritual into your life. What everyday rituals would you like to craft? What are the bigger life moments you'd like to honour? What elements are important for you to incorporate into your rituals? Is it ancestor work, nature elements, working with moon phases or the cycles of the year? Would you like to carry out these rituals alone or invite others to join in? What books could you use to draw inspiration from?

Honour Your Innate Rhythm

Another way to honour our cyclical nature would be to keep track of daily energy levels. After a few months of this, you should be able to see if there are any repeating patterns, such as hormonal patterns. With this information, you can plot future activities so that they take full advantage of your energy levels. If you notice there are certain days every month that you are high energy and enthusiastic, then this is the time to book in meetings, new activities, social gatherings and travel. If you notice certain periods of time that you are low in mood and energy, try to schedule in minimal activities and focus on rest and self-care on these days instead.

You can also take your cue from nature. If it's raining, stormy, or snowing, perhaps this is the day to stay cosied up inside. Take the day to retreat and turn inward. Tone down your activities and hibernate as much as possible during winter. For me, winter is a season for napping, spending time reading and researching, and making time to journal and pull cards. It's a time to conserve energy, reflect on what has and hasn't been working and seek answers from inside myself. I also like to give myself time each month to incorporate a few days of pure rest and reflection as well; it's good for my soul and makes me a nicer person to be around! We give ourselves a gift when we honour our natural rhythms, and we remind ourselves we are part of and connected to nature and not separate from the ecosystems around us.

Tuning into our rhythms has an added effect of amplifying our intuition. We are able to hear our bodies speak much more easily when we have times of quiet reflection. We have time to look for messages in our surroundings and to pay attention to dreams when we aren't racing from place to place or being buried in mountains of work. Life is more enjoyable when we have time to create daily rituals, to meditate, to pray, to sing and to take time to appreciate the beauty around us.

Life will always offer us more. It will always be filled with so much to experience and so much asking for our attention. It is up to us to remember that we are worthy of time and attention too. It is up to us to remember how much more aligned and clear we feel when we are able to carve out space for ourselves. Try to do a few things each day that are just for you. It could be starting the day with lighting a candle and burning incense so you can bless and anoint yourself as you get ready for work. It could be journaling and pulling cards before bed. Find what works for you and do more of it! The world needs more people in tune with their magic and medicine.

Exercise

Keep a journal for at least the next month and note down the following:

- How you feel with specific weather patterns:
  - Do rainy, cloudy days make you feel gloomy?
  - Do you have more energy on sunny days?
  - Are there specific activities or foods you crave during the different weather?
- How does the cycle of the moon affect you?
  - Do certain phases energise you or cause you to feel drained and tired?
- What seasons do you love and why?
- What seasons do you not like and why?
- What activities or foods do you like to indulge in during each season?
- What times of the day do you feel energised? When do you feel tired?

Armed with the information you have collected, you can then use this to help you better schedule your time and incorporate activities and practices that take full advantage of when you need to rest and reflect, or when you are energised and ready to create and explore!

EPILOGUE/
AFTERWORD

"You had the power all along my dear."
~ *Glinda, the Good Witch in Wizard of Oz* ~

In *The Miracle Club: How Thoughts Become Reality*, Mitch Horowitz talks about the idea of choosing a book that contains certain ethical and spiritual ideas and dedicating a chunk of time to fully immersing yourself in it; he suggests 9 months.[11] Use this time to live and breathe a certain idea and principle. Does this idea and way of life enhance who you are and the way you show up? See if it provides you with comfort and clarity, if it challenges you to do better and be better. See if it falls short or even if the book and its ideas prove to be entirely wrong for you and your way of life.

Mitch is talking about great works such as *Bhagavad Gita* and *Tao Te Ching*, and also the ideas of authors such as Viktor Frankl. There's strong merit in applying commitment and trying out new ideas for a chunk of time. We often read a book, resonate with its ideas and then put it away and move on to the next book or course, looking for something else to consume to fill the hole of longing inside ourselves. I know I have done this many times myself!

Instead, I invite you to lean into any ideas in this book that may have really resonated with you. Lean in, commit to it and make them your own. Flavour the rituals with your own beliefs and personality, embellish them with more, call in deities, and try circle casting, or strip them back to the bare bones if a more minimalist approach is your thing.

Practise those ideas; really relish working on healing and celebrating all the multifaceted goodness that is you. In doing so, you will find the path back home to you. You will find a whole world of mystery, wonder, connection, strength, love and beauty in the shadow and the light that is you.

It is also so important, as you walk this path, to remain open-minded – we do not know it all. We will grow and evolve and change. Try not to fall into the trap of a rigid mindset and of needing to be right. There is so much to learn and it is more than okay to make mistakes, to stumble and fall. This is how we grow. Read and learn from various sources – not just the opinions you agree with, but also read and learn from the other side of the coin as well. This is how we build robust knowledge and how we learn compassion and understanding.

It's worthwhile pointing out that in today's world, where we have a sense of immediacy about everything, that spiritual work takes time. It takes time to learn, grow and heal. It takes time to find the right teachers and mentors, whether they be people, plants, or books. It's also okay to outgrow your mentors, or to only need them for a short amount of time before moving onto another mentor better suited to your current needs. You can use your discernment and decide that something or someone is no longer right for you. I believe that this is the most beautiful part of the human existence, the never-ending potential for learning, for expansion and for healing ourselves.

When you work on yourself, when you commit to healing, learning and growing, examining your thoughts, taking radical self-responsibility, and to showing up for yourself consistently, it is inevitable that you will encounter bumps along the way. Those nagging inner thoughts of not being enough that stem from those core childhood wounds and any other issues will all bob up to the surface. Don't push them back down again; don't run away. Instead, pick them up, examine them and see what they have to teach you.

Practise the level of love and empathy you would have for others with yourself. Celebrate the beautiful moments; seek out the wonder and the humour that is available for you. Lean in – there is so much to learn here on our journeys. There is so much to share and there are so many threads of connection to make, with all of our kin: human, non-human and spirit.

Practise what resonates with you. Put in the effort and lean in with love. When you walk this path, your journey will inevitably lead you to remember the truth we are all born with, but easily forget: all the magic and the medicine you ever needed was right here, inside you, all along.

So welcome home, lovely soul. Thank you for sharing the journey with me. May many blessings come your way.

JOURNAL

ABOUT THE AUTHOR

Jayne is lovingly known as a "Wellness Witch" – a clinically trained and magically minded holistic health practitioner and coach.

Jayne is formally trained in Naturopathy and Herbal Medicine and is also qualified in Aromascience and as a Postnatal Doula. She has over 25 years' experience in tarot reading and earth-based spirituality, fusing her practical skills and holistic health knowledge with ritual and spiritual coaching.

Jayne is passionate about supporting and empowering women as they journey home to their most authentic selves and rediscover their own inner magic and medicine. Jayne has appeared on several international podcasts and is the founder of Magic & Medicine, a New Zealand based company focused on health, healing, herbs, self-care and spirituality.

You can connect with Jayne at:

magicandmedicine.co.nz

@magicandmedicine_ on Instagram

ACKNOWLEDGEMENTS

A special thanks to the following people who have enriched my life in ways I can never fully express.

My Grandma, who gave me a deep love of books, history and the written word. My Grandad, who gifted me the appreciation of imagination and sharing stories. My parents who raised, loved and supported me through the ups and downs of life. My brother, whose humour and understanding has helped me through some hard times.

My other mother Jan, whose faith and encouragement has always been so unwavering; it was Jan who told me never to let anyone steal my magic.

My four amazing children, Finn, Savannah, Anika and Sebastian who never cease to bring me love, joy and wonder, you are all changing the world for the better just by being in it. Thank you for choosing me to be your mum.

My mentor and friend Erika, who helped set me on this path of accountability and healing. Erika led by example and paved a way for me to show up and dream big.

Mark, Todd and Joyce who have backed me every step of the way, gifting me with family and friendship.

My witchy soul sister Laura, who has been with me holding my hand along the way. Encouraging me, talking me through moments of self-doubt and offering her amazing insight.

Big love to Eilish and Amanda, whose connection and encouragement has kept me going.

And to the team at Dean Publishing, you have all been incredible to work with and made this dream a reality.

Massive love and thanks to YOU for picking up this book and allowing me into your life.

~ Jaynie

Endnotes

1   Goyal M, Singh S, Sibinga EMS, et al. 'Meditation Programs for Psychological Stress and Well-being: A Systematic Review and Meta-analysis.' *JAMA Intern Med.* 2014;174(3):357–368. doi:10.1001/jamainternmed.2013.13018

2   Lee, M. S., Lee, J., Park, B. J., & Miyazaki, Y. (2015). 'Interaction with indoor plants may reduce psychological and physiological stress by suppressing autonomic nervous system activity in young adults: a randomized crossover study.' *Journal of physiological anthropology*, 34(1), 21. https://doi.org/10.1186/s40101-015-0060-8

3   Battaglia, S. (2003). *The complete guide to aromatherapy.* Brisbane: International Centre of Holistic Aromatherapy.

4   Hansen, Margaret M et al. 'Shinrin-Yoku (Forest Bathing) and Nature Therapy: A State-of-the-Art Review.' *International journal of environmental research and public health* vol. 14,8 851. 28 Jul. 2017, doi:10.3390/ijerph14080851

5   NASA (2019) 'NASA Plant Research Offers a Breath of Fresh Air', published online https://spinoff.nasa.gov/Spinoff2019/cg_7.html

6   Radin, D., Hayssen, G., Emoto, M., & Kizu, T. (2006). 'Double-blind test of the effects of distant intention on water crystal formation.'

Explore (New York, N.Y.), 2(5), 408–411. https://doi.org/10.1016/j.explore.2006.06.004

7   Emoto, Masaru, 1943-2014. (2004). *The Hidden Messages in Water*. Hillsboro, Or. : [Emeryville, CA] :Beyond Words Pub. ; Distributed to the trade by Publishers Group West,

8   *The Encyclopedia of Bach flower Therapy* (1999). Healing Arts Press; Vermont, p 25.

9   Serpeloni, F., Radtke, K., de Assis, S. et al. 'Grandmaternal stress during pregnancy and DNA methylation of the third generation: an epigenome-wide association study'. *Transl Psychiatry* 7, e1202 (2017). https://doi.org/10.1038/tp.2017.153

10 Murphy, Amantha. (31 January 2021). *The Way of the Seabhean: An Irish Shamanic*, Womancraft Publishing, pp. 200.

11 Horowitz, Mitch. (1 December 2019), *The Miracle Club: How Thoughts Become Reality*, Inner Traditions Illustrated edition.

www.ingramcontent.com/pod-product-compliance
Lightning Source LLC
Chambersburg PA
CBHW022052020426
42335CB00012B/662